Dec 23/17

To Wendy & Doug

BOATS IN MY BLOOD

Best Wishes

"Barrie"

Thanks for the wine
and the hospitality + songs
. "Cheers"

We sing well together
love Barrie

BOATS
IN
MY BLOOD

A Life in Boat Building

BARRIE FARRELL

HARBOUR PUBLISHING

Harbour Publishing Co. Ltd.
P.O. Box 219, Madeira Park, BC, V0N 2H0
www.harbourpublishing.com

Edited by Peter Robson
Copyedited by Patricia Wolfe
Indexed by Brianna Cerkiewicz
Cover design by Diane Robertson
Text design by Mary White
Photos courtesy Barrie Farrell except where otherwise noted
Printed and bound in Canada on FSC-certifed paper containing
    30% post-consumer recycled content

Harbour Publishing acknowledges the support of the Canada
Council for the Arts, which last year invested $157 million
to bring the arts to Canadians throughout the country.
We also gratefully acknowledge financial support from the
Government of Canada through the Canada Book Fund and
from the Province of British Columbia through the BC Arts
Council and the Book Publishing Tax Credit.

Cataloguing data available from Library and Archives Canada
ISBN 978-1-55017-755-8 (paper)
ISBN 978-1-55017-756-5 (ebook)

Contents

Foreword

Brian Lee

They were the first boats I recall admiring. My dad's boat, the *Sedna*, was a Penson—a plywood gillnetter built in Pender Harbour the year I was born. It was fast and a great little boat, but I felt pangs of disloyalty to her every time we'd pass one of those new Farrells. Their crown-like dodgers made them stand out from the other flat-topped silhouettes on the grounds and I enjoyed the curves of their flared bow and ample, rounded stern. They held your eye, drawing attention along proud, graceful lines. They were sexy.

At the time, I didn't even know their builder started out in my hometown of Pender Harbour. It was there in 1966 that Barrie Farrell built his first "bigger" boat, the *Klyuhk,* and finished it off with a layer of fibreglass over its plywood hull. That boat is now the *Gotta Go* and can still be seen regularly cruising around the harbour.

Not long after, Farrell popped his first fibreglass mould off another glass-over-wood boat, the thirty-four-foot *Alice R.*

"I just figured it out," he told me with his characteristic nonchalance.

"I just waxed it up good and it all popped off fine."

By 1974 he owned a shop in Richmond and built fifty boats from a new thirty-seven-foot mould in one year. That's on top of the orders he had for his twenty-seven- and twenty-nine-footers. Soon he took the twenty-nine-foot design and made it into a thirty-two-footer.

To my six-year-old eyes they made the other flattish-hulled plywood gillnetters seem kind of homely. They were also faster than most with clean decks and fittings that didn't look like a fisherman had installed them. They brought a pleasure boat esthetic to a commercial industry that rarely concerned itself with looks.

That's not to say there weren't beautiful fishboats already bobbing around out there. Later on I'd come to appreciate other builders like Gooldrup, Wahl or Frostad but the Farrells always stood out for me.

Commercial fishermen are utilitarian creatures who value square usefulness and don't always adopt new ways easily. So it's a testament to the quality of the Farrell boat that word of mouth sparked an enormous demand in a very short time. The Farrells became the most popular boat ever to break into BC's commercial fishing industry.

They were at the forefront of a boat building revolution in which lighter, faster hulls could suddenly be mass produced. Fibreglass boats required much less maintenance than their wooden sisters and despite early concerns by wood holdouts, they were durable. And Barrie Farrell's timing was perfect, coming along at a time when fishing regulations rewarded speed.

The fact that he went broke a couple of times despite enormous success points to the reality that, like many of the names in BC's boat building log book, he was a better builder than he was a businessman. But history rarely concerns itself with how much money was earned or lost. Farrell is recognized as a rare type—someone who possesses both an eye for bold design and the practical tools to make them work. He built more than three hundred boats in his career and there are well over three hundred more that boast his distinctive hull or cabin. Other boat builders floated their own names on hulls popped off a Farrell mould—and likely built an equal number—yet provided minimal or no compensation or acknowledgement to their designer.

But Barrie Farrell isn't bitter about that, nor is he finished with boats. At the age of eighty-one, he's still working. I called him up yesterday and as the phone rang, I pictured him watching reruns of *Bonanza* from his favourite chair at home in Nanaimo. It didn't surprise me at all when he told me he was over in Tofino buffing away on some guy's boat. A lifetime spent sanding fibreglass and teak doesn't usually prescribe a healthy old age but on any given week he might be in

Pender Harbour, Comox, Nanaimo or Parksville still doing just that.

Moving around seems to suit him. Barrie Farrell has rarely stayed put in the same spot for long and it's shown in the number of friends he's made all over the coast. But it's his reputation as a perfectionist that points to why his skills are still in demand. When he is home he scratches out new designs and says he's got a pleasure boat in him yet.

"People still buy these ugly-looking things from the States. These modern boats, the newer they are the worse they get," he told me once.

"I think the manufacturers are having a contest to see who can build the ugliest boat—rounded off, no decks, squinty windows, nothing lining up, so high and ugly.

"Oh man, they're just terrible."

He's drawn up plans for a forty-foot cruiser.

"It looks more like a tugboat than these other ones they call tugs, you know—like Nordic Tugs.

"I always wanted to build it but it's just a dream now."

Maybe, but Barrie Farrell's legacy will float on in the number of his boats—whether they carry his name or not—that still work and play on the coast. And, if you ever get the pleasure of chatting with this soft-spoken gentleman, you'll find he's just fine with that.

—Brian Lee is editor of the *Harbour Spiel*
in Madeira Park, BC

1

The Early Years

When I was born in North Vancouver on November 16, 1934, my parents named me Darrell Malory Daniels. My father's name—at that time—was Malory Jasper Daniels and my mom's name was Betty Daniels. About a dozen years later, my dad was persuaded to become a Kabalarian (a philosophy dealing with numbers and names) and changed our last names to Farrell. We all got to pick our first names, but we didn't use middle names. Dad changed his to Allen Farrell, my brother Jerry's to Rob (but he later stuck with Jerry), brother Patrick became Keray and I became Barrie.

We lived in a squatter's shack that Dad built on the flats east of Lynmore just above the Second Narrows bridge in North Vancouver. That was in the hungry thirties. Dad used to frequent the gym and practise

*My dad, Allen, around the time
he went to Victoria and won the
prize for best overall BC athlete.*

gymnastics, and when a sports competition came along in Victoria (sort of a mini Olympics), Dad came in first as the all-round BC athlete and right away got a job in Chilliwack as a gym instructor. We rented a house in Chilliwack but it was built up off the ground about ten feet. In the winter the cold wind whistled under it and the water pipes froze a lot, so Dad spent a lot of time under the house with a blowtorch thawing pipes. That's when Dad got the dream in his head about building a boat and sailing to the tropics.

During the winter he built a couple of twelve-foot rowboats in the living room. His plan was to build one for him and one for my mom so they could go hand trolling for salmon in the summer. The boats were planked, slightly V-bottomed with square sterns, different from the traditional double-ended handline boats of the time and not the easiest to row.

In the spring, when I was just over a year old, my brother Jerry was born and when school was over, Dad and Mom loaded all their stuff in the two boats. Jerry and I rode along in apple boxes, one of us in each boat. Our parents started rowing down the Fraser River on their way north to Lasqueti Island near the top end of the Strait of Georgia, and began hand trolling for salmon. It was a long row and took about four days and nights. Dad had rigged up a little sail but there was either no wind or it was blowing in the wrong direction, so when they got to the north corner of Scottie Bay they had a good rest before they started fishing up around the Fegen Islets at the north end of Lasqueti.

At that time, a fellow called Pete Dubois was the fish buyer. He was living on Lasqueti, but later moved to Pender Harbour. He was going from boat to boat every day collecting the fish with his thirty-four-foot packer *Susan D*.

They fished most of the summer around Lasqueti and the Ballenas Islands (where there were lots of rabbits, so we ate a lot of them) and then headed down to Nanoose Bay to wait for the winter run of spring salmon to show up. Dad built a cabin on a little island in a lagoon in or near Nanoose Bay. We squatted there and he

My mother, Betty, with a day's catch from hand trolling. She was high boat that day, catching the most fish.

fell a tree and started chopping out a keel for his tropics dream boat.

We soon ran out of money so Dad rowed down to Nanaimo and went to the relief office to see what he could do. He wanted to go to work on the road or do anything for some money, but the guy there said, "No, I can't give you a job or any money because you haven't been here six months." Dad said, "Look mister, I've got a wife and two kids and we're out of food so I'm not leaving here until I get something." He slammed the door on his way out and sat on the steps to cool down. The guy from the office came out after a while and said, "Okay, take this slip and go and see the foreman on the road crew in the morning and he'll put you to work."

Dad worked there for a couple of months, but it was a long row between the cabin and work, plus the days were getting shorter and the weather bad. He had to row in the dark through some bad storms and it finally got to him. One day he said, "Okay, you guys, let's get the heck out of here." So we rowed to the head of Nanoose Bay and he was lucky as there were some guys on the beach and he asked them if they wanted to buy our rowboats for a low price, and one of the men bought them. We left the tropics' keel unfinished, packed up and walked up to the Red Gap store where we were able to catch a ride down to Nanaimo. We slept in a park overnight and the next day caught the CPR boat to Vancouver and back over to the flats in North Vancouver, where our little shack was still waiting for us.

We had some interesting neighbours. There was big Jim Warburton, who had sailed around Cape Horn several times on the old square-riggers. He was a big man with a ruddy complexion and monstrous hands. He had a wealth of knowledge in boat building and was my dad's mentor. Then there was Malcolm Lowry, "the poet Lowry," who was famous for his poetry and writing, and also did some acting and spent quite a bit of time in Hollywood. But he had a bad drinking problem. Another was Scotty Neish, who was also a boat builder and fisherman. Scotty later became an organizer and respected leader in the United Fishermen and Allied Workers' Union (UFAWU). All three had progressive ideas and helped Dad develop egalitarian values (equality for all people) and humane thinking, which he valued all through his life.

Dad got a job in a sawmill and built a big shed to build a new boat. Over the next year he built a thirty-six-foot troller named *South Wind* and in the spring we headed up the coast to go trolling. We made it to Pender Harbour and Dad tried fishing out of there, but the old car engine he had put in wouldn't run right, so he ended up hand trolling out of the dingy.

Mom and Dad thought they would like to sell the boat and buy some property in Pender Harbour, so they went looking and found a little log house just outside of Bargain Bay. They put a down payment on it and fixed it up, added new curtains and all. They were able to sell the boat, but they had to run it to Vancouver. We got it there, but with difficulty. They came back with the money for

In his spare time, while living on the flats in North Vancouver, Dad built a thirty-six-foot troller named South Wind *in the shed to the left. He also built this little play boat. That's me holding the mast, with brother Jerry.*

the house, but when they tried to go into the house an English couple named Blye came to the door and said, "Get out of here, we bought this place and everything here is ours." I don't think we ever got our deposit back. What a disappointment, but actually the creeps did us a favour because we found a beautiful piece of sheltered waterfront property right in Bargain Bay with good, deep water and a nice tidal lagoon on one side. It was five acres of well-timbered land and Dad bought it for $180. He had the back part of it logged off by a well-known local logger, Ole Kleven, and made $200. This was in 1938.

We lived in a tent while Dad built a house, but when it went on into winter it got awfully cold. I remember the icicles pretty close to my nose when I woke up. I love the smell of woodsmoke. It always brings back fond memories of the old campfire outside the tent. Mom would cook up some amazing meals on it and we would all huddle around it to keep warm and have little sing-songs. Dad built the house out of cedar poles off the property and cedar shakes. I used to go with him beachcombing for good cedar slabs to cut shingle bolts for the shakes. The house was still standing up until about 2012 and it was still sound when they tore it down.

Brother Jerry clowning around with friend Donald Scoular (the handsome guy in the background) in front of our old house in Bargain Harbour. We sold that house to Russ Keillor.

There were no roads and hardly any trails back then so the only way to get around was by boat. All we had was the little dinghy that Dad had kept off the *South Wind*. Once a week, the Union Steamship would arrive at Irvines Landing with passengers and freight. Boat Day was a big event and we'd row the five miles to Irvines and sit on the hard timbers on the edge of the dock to watch all the action.

Dad and me used go out cod fishing in that little thing and he'd tie a line through the fishes' gills and tow them behind to keep them alive, then he'd put them in a live tank when we got home and sell them once a week.

After a while we got moved into the house and Dad built a boat shed where he built a sixteen-foot, double-end open cod boat with live tanks and an air-cooled Wisconsin engine in her. Dad built a few rowboats for people and cod fished, but we never had much money.

The Brown family moved to Bargain Harbour from Nanaimo, towing a house, which they pulled up on the property across the lagoon from us. Now we had a young playmate (Norman), but his mother was pretty straight-laced and didn't like him playing with the heathens across the way too much. We used to run around bare-naked all summer, which reminds me of the day Jerry got stung right on the end of his pee-pee and went around with a woody for the rest of the day.

Waiting for the tide to get high enough to let us through Canoe Pass on our way home from Boat Day at Irvines Landing. The floats belonging to Dary Carter's boat works are in the background. I'm in the stern with Mom, Jerry is in the bow and Dad is at the oars.

They were good days at Bargain Harbour, especially in the summer. It was a great place for kids to grow up. We were in and out of the water all day. We had a whole fleet of model boats. We would have them on a long stick with a string tied to the boat and we could make them go like hell or just cruise. We'd go tree climbing and build forts.

One of us would get to go cod fishing with Dad, but when we got our own little seven-foot rowboats, we made up our own set lines and would fish for rock cod. We ate healthy: lots of vegetables from the garden and lots of fish, but not much meat.

A guy bought property on the other side of us and built a house. He was a schoolteacher by the name of Hildege (I'm not sure of the spelling) and he taught school at Silver Sands, but he wasn't a very nice man. He was hated at school and he was the only man I ever saw my dad argue with and pretty near come to blows. We were in our rowboat and he was on the shore and they started talking then arguing then shouting. Hildege picked up a 2x4 and Dad grabbed an oar. I was scared there was going to be war but Dad finally said, "Ah, go to hell, you're not worth the effort," and we left. The school didn't like him either and he left after one season. A fellow named Tommy Thomas bought his house. They had a son named Brian. He was a little older than us, but we had another playmate. (Years later, Tommy moved to Parksville on Vancouver Island and had a used car lot right across from where Mom and her boyfriend, Ralph, had rented a house.) As we all had our own little rowboats, we would have races. Sometimes when it was blowing a howling southeaster we'd head outside the harbour in our little boats and ride the big waves (Dad didn't know). Dinghies actually ride the waves pretty good, but watch out for the big curlers! There was Norman, Brian, my brother Jerry and me chumming around together and on school days we would row across the bay and walk the four-mile trail to the Maple Leaf school at Donley Landing.

When I think back on our school days at the Maple Leaf, things were pretty hilarious. There was a certain amount of bullying that went on, but mostly it was all in fun. One favourite was for a couple of the bigger kids to climb up a sapling and bend it down to the ground, then put one of us little guys on the top of the tree and "let 'er go." If you didn't hang on tight as you could, you'd probably have gone sailing through the air into the woods.

Then there was an old, abandoned, dry well that they would throw us down until they were ready to help us out. Sometimes when things got carried away and it turned into bullying, Frank Campbell, one of the big guys, would step in and put a stop to it (he was our hero). One of the big guys (no names mentioned) had a mean streak in him. The bullies used to pick on poor old Norm Brown a lot. We used to have pine cone fights and occasionally we'd get carried away and start throwing anything handy: sticks, hunks of wood and sometimes even rocks.

Another sport on the way home when we got to the Scoulars' field was dried horse bun fights. There would be the Douglas (Reggie and Stanley) and Scoular kids (Donald and Davie) against us Bargain Harbour guys. At times someone might get a little upset and let go with a fresh one.

There's a bush that grows wild. I think its proper name is spirea. We called it buckshit and we used to smoke it. We would dampen down brown paper and roll up a big one. Sometimes the paper would dry out and burn our eyebrows off.

Anyway, all in all, it was a good school. We had dandy sports days there too. They'd go all afternoon with free ice cream (on dry ice) and hot dogs, and then a dance in the evening.

Harold Whalen worked at the store at Donley Landing—it was owned by a fellow named Gill Mervin at the time—and he would ride his motorcycle to work from his house at the mouth of Bargain Harbour. Along the way he'd have to ride past the Scoulars' field. The Scoulars had a big white horse in their field and Harold liked to chase the horse a bit in this big open field. One day Harold parked the bike on the trail and went down to have a look at a new boat a Japanese fishing family, the Kawasakis, were building. They also built big beautiful burl furniture. The father was quite the craftsman. While they were down there they heard a heck of a racket out on the trail so they ran out there to see what it was. The horse had wandered along the trail and spotted the bike, went over to it and kicked the hell out of it.

Another time Dad and me were walking the trail and as we passed the Scoulars', Bill, the dad, was out working in the yard and Dad and him got talking over the fence. Bill said, "I just finished installing one of them new-fangled flushing toilets in the house and I don't know if that's good or bad, we used to at least go outside to the outhouse to take a big smelly shit, but now," he said, "we shit right in the house."

Another pastime we had was fishing perch, shiners and rock cod off the float in front of our place and the floats at Donley Landing. We could sell the perch and rock cod, but the shiners were just for fun. Those little guys are hard to catch because they are experts at stealing the bait, but I outsmarted them about ten years ago (I was still a kid at heart) and started using a herring jig. A herring jig is just a bunch of empty hooks with coloured thread dangling off a weighted line. Pretty well every time I pulled it up, it was loaded with shiners. It seems like cheating in a way, but I guess all the fishing nowadays is with all the sophisticated electronics and methods of finding fish.

My brother Jerry was a perfect swimmer and diver at the age of four and I didn't learn till the next year, so age-wise I was two years behind him. Our friend Colin Hanney and his friend came in and tied up to our float in Bargain Harbour in a beautiful little twenty-one-foot sailboat that Colin had just built called *Balandra*. Anyway, him and his buddy got a kick out of throwing money in for Jerry to dive for and they kept throwing the coins in deeper and deeper and were amazed how deep he could go. That boat is still around and still owned by Colin's wife, Shendra.

Dad built himself a twenty-four-foot cod boat with a four-horsepower Easthope. She was a well-built, good, solid boat with a gumwood stem, keel and horn timber and lots of other gumwood throughout. She had yellow cedar ribs so they wouldn't rot like oak does. She had the best of material all through. Dad named her *Kivi*, which means "rock" in some other language— Finnish, I think. These days

Me bottom painting the Kivi *with brother Keray in the foreground, 1945. I was eleven years old.*

The Kivi *with Dad at the helm.*

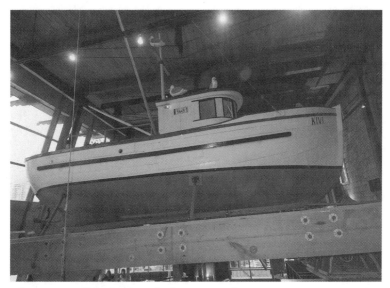

The Kivi *is still looking good after seventy-five years.* PHOTO COURTESY ALAN
HAIG-BROWN

she is hanging in a fancy seafood restaurant called the
Sandbar at Granville Island in Vancouver.

When *Kivi* was complete Dad sold the sixteen-foot
double-ender cod boat to St. Mary's Hospital in Garden
Bay, Pender Harbour. As there weren't many roads, they
used it for getting around the harbour.

As I mentioned, Union Steamship day at Irvines
Landing was a big day. There was usually a dozen or
two people on the dock to pick up freight, send it, pick
up people off the boat, catch the boat to Vancouver or
just visit on the dock. One day just before Christmas,
Dad and me went over to meet the boat and as she was
backing out she kept on going and backed right up on
the Indian Islands near the mouth of the harbour. All the
bigger fishboats hooked on and tried to pull her off but

Boat Day at Irvines Landing, 1949. A Union steamship is approaching the dock. PHOTO COURTESY LINDA MATTIS

no luck (the bigger boats in those days weren't very big). The captain and crew might have been into the Christmas cheer. They had to get a big tug to pull them off and tow them to Vancouver.

Jim Warburton, our neighbour when we lived on the flats in North Vancouver, showed up at Bargain Harbour one day. He was heading north, fishing in his little gill-netter with a small square wheelhouse just big enough to get your head in (you just kind of wore it). Anyway, as I mentioned earlier, Jim taught Dad a lot of tricks about boat building, like how to make his own paint and putty with powdered whiting, linseed oil and pigment. While Dad and Mom and Jim were sitting visiting at the kitchen table, and Jerry and me were playing upstairs, an earthquake happened. When it first started, Dad shouted up at us, "Hey, you kids take it easy up there." Then, after a few seconds, he shouted up again, "For god sakes, you guys, cut it out." The whole house started to shake and you could hear boat lumber falling out of the rafters in the boat shed across the bay. Somewhere, a woman was screaming. Everybody ran outside except Jim. He just sat there, and when we all came back in he says, "Oh ya, that'll be your earthquake. Now where was I? Oh ya, I married an Indian girl and we had a baby. We were way out in the sticks with no doctors available, so I put a blanket on the kitchen table, laid her down and helped the baby out. Then when the little guy was out I hauled out my jackknife and cut the little bugger adrift."

Christmas 1940. As she was backing out from Irvines Landing, the Union steamship Lady Cecelia *kept on going and backed right up on the Skardon Islands near the mouth of the harbour.* PHOTO #1200 COURTESY SUNSHINE COAST MUSEUM & ARCHIVES

Dad limbed a big tree behind the house and bought a new piece of three-quarter-inch rope and hung it about seventy feet up, so we had big Tarzan swing. There was a big old fallen tree with the big roots sticking way up in the air, so we could climb up there and whistle through the air, hair straight back, up high. One day, our neighbour buddy Norm came to swing with us and he swung off a lower stump and held on to the rope fairly low, so when he came in for a landing he was too low to the ground, where there were a bunch of little stumps sticking up. He kept lifting his legs up higher and higher with them kind of spread out so his crotch was pretty vulnerable and, *womp*, he straddled a stump. Man, was he hurting! Although it looked kind of funny and it was hard not to laugh, the poor guy was really hurt, so we helped him up and he went hobbling down the trail as fast as he could go, holding his crotch and hollering, "Daddy! Daddy!"

Salmon Arm

When I was ten years old, my aunt (Dad's sister) had a good friend whose dad, Mr. Salter, had a big fruit orchard near Notch Hill, north of Salmon Arm in the interior of BC. She arranged for me to go up there to pick cherries, so Dad put me on the Union Steamship and I met Aunt Billy in Vancouver. She put me on the train and the Salters picked me up at the other end. The Salters had a nice daughter my age—Wendy—and we became good friends. They had a couple of horses and we would go riding together up in the hills. I picked cherries for a while, but I wasn't very good at it so they got me building the wooden boxes for the cherries and I was good at that. I'm still building boxes, but they have a motor in them and they float.

Bing and Tychy

One time I was getting bark for firewood at the back of our property in the harbour and I was prying the bark off an old snag with a long pole when a big piece came down and landed on my ankle awfully hard. I couldn't walk on it, so I crawled back home and down to the float where Dad was visiting some friends, Bing and Tychy, who had come on their boat to visit for a few weeks. Tychy was a psychic and a healer and she said just lie on the bunk and I'll fix you up. She rubbed my ankle quite a bit and then waved her hands over it for a long time and mumbled a bunch of strange words. When I stood up I could walk just fine.

Another time Bing and Tychy went to Vancouver for a couple of days and Tychy asked Dad to look after her cats. One was a nice, cuddly, purring cat and the other was a big, tough, square-jawed, mean old Manx tomcat with attitude, named Baby. One night Baby was outside our house yowling like a banshee and Dad went out and threw a couple of rocks at it to shut it up. The next day after Bing and Tychy got home, Tychy said to Dad, "I'm disappointed in you, Allen. Baby told me you threw rocks at him." Now, there was no way anybody could have known that Dad threw rocks at the cat in the middle of the night in a secluded place like ours, but Tychy knew.

Back on the Flats

In 1943, my youngest brother, Keray, was born. It was that year that my mom and dad split up. Dad kept Keray (who was to remain with him the entire time he was growing up) and Jerry and me went to live with Mom at our Aunt Lois's place out on the flats on Mountain Highway, below the Lynnwood Hotel in North Vancouver. Jerry and me went to Keith Lynn school and Mom worked at Uncle Henry's cafe, called Henry's Hamburger. It was in the corner of the parking lot at the old Lynnwood Hotel. The main road used to go down around the bottom (south side) of the hotel.

One day I took a spill off my bike and banged up my leg pretty good. I didn't tell anybody and it got infected. It got so bad I got big lumps under my arms and couldn't walk one morning when I got up. Mom was at work, so I crawled up the gravel road to Uncle Henry's and he took me to the Vancouver General Hospital. There they put me in bed and proceeded to pump me full of penicillin. The syringes for the penicillin back then had pretty big needles (in my memory they seemed to be about a foot long). Anyway, they kept me in for about a week and I pulled through okay. It was a bad case of blood poisoning.

Pender Island

When summer holidays came, Jerry and me went over to our granddad Jasper Daniels' farm on Pender Island, in the Gulf Islands. It was pretty good there during the summer. There were fruit trees, a horse to ride and we enjoyed helping Grandpa with the haying and chores around the farm. We did lots of eating fruit, chasing chickens, riding the horse and going down to Hope Bay for a swim and row around in the little boat Gramps kept there.

Then came the fall and Gramps had to go to Vancouver to work, so he left us in the care of his girl-friend, Mary Mathison. The whole scene wasn't much fun anymore. We had to pretty well take over all the chores around the farm. When the days got short we were up early in the morning while it was still dark and packed water in twenty-litre pails from the house at the front of the property up to the barn. We wouldn't fill them right up, but we would fill them as full as we could and still be able to pack them. We would milk the cow, clean the barn, feed all the animals, pack in the wood, then have breakfast and get ready for school. There were always more chores when we got home.

Mary was very, very strict with us and she had a violent temper, which she used often. She would put a lot of cod liver oil on our porridge and make us eat it, but she calmed down in the evenings and when we went to bed she would read us stories. I remember Huckleberry Finn polling down the Mississippi River. I would shut my eyes and visualize Huck and his buddy, Jim, polling along with the bright moon and stars shining in the dark blue sky, the orange glow of the campfire in the sandbox on the log raft and the bright reflection of lights on the water—all in vivid Technicolor!

Then one night Jerry said, "To hell with this BS, let's blow this zoo!" So we decided to run away. We packed our packsacks, grabbed our sleeping bags and headed out. We walked for a couple of hours then went in to this farm where there was an old abandoned chicken coop. We went in, spread out our sleeping bags and stretched out. In the wee hours of the morning, the farmer saw our flashlight. He came out and said, "What the hell are you guys up to?" So we told him and he took us into his house and we stretched out in the warmth and slept for a couple of hours. We had breakfast with the farmer then he drove us back to our farm and came into the house with us to have a talk with Mary. She was better for a while, but then she went right back to being her hotheaded self.

When we went back to Mom's place in North Vancouver for Christmas, we told her and Uncle Henry how Mary was treating us, so Mom decided not to send us back. (Poor old Mary, I think we exaggerated quite a bit.) So it was back to Keith Lynn school.

Back in North Vancouver

It was a pretty cold winter and all the little ponds were frozen over, so we went ice-skating a lot. One day I got in a fight with a kid on the ice and we fought for the longest time, both dead even. There was blood all over the ice but we kept clubbing it out. We were both beat, but we kept going at it till we could hardly stand up. We finally realized it was no use and called a truce. I never saw the kid again, but sure remembered it as I had two black eyes for quite a while and also a broken nose.

Pender Harbour

About the end of February, I went back up to Bargain Harbour and lived with Dad for the rest of the school season, and went to the old Maple Leaf school at Donley Landing.

All my old buddies were there, and there was a big kid named Walter Higgins. We got in a disagreement and I challenged him to fight. He was bigger and stronger than me but I was faster and I won the fight. A week or so later, I'm still kind of cocky so I challenge him to another fight and I won again. Same thing on the third fight. It became a regular event, the kids all watching Walt and me fight. But the fourth fight was a little different. We fought for a long time, and I just about had him—his nose and teeth were bleeding, but we were both slowing down. I sure wasn't as fast as usual and all of a sudden I saw his big fist coming at me and I couldn't duck fast enough. The last thing I remember Walt saying as the big fist came at me was "Poor guy," and then I was out cold. Served me right. Walt was a pretty nice guy actually, sort of a gentle giant.

All the schools' sports days were combined into one field and held at the Maple Leaf school. One of the kids, Benny Dubois, could have been an amazing athlete. When we had our sports days, he would win every event he was in—in his own grade—and then he would go into competition with the high school guys and win all those events too. He was also a good boat builder at a young age. He designed and built a nice fifteen-foot speedboat when he was sixteen or seventeen years old. He put a V4

Wisconsin engine in her. It was a pretty little boat with an alternating red and yellow cedar deck varnished up the same as the ones I was to build. Benny and me were going to go into partnership, but he went logging and beachcombing instead.

I had a few more fights at different schools I went to but I finally became wiser and more humane and realized fighting and war were for the birds, especially these wars nowadays that are all about power, greed and oil, where thousands and thousands of innocent people get slaughtered just so a few people can get richer. So I kind of became a pacifist. But I sort of went against my principles a couple of summers ago when I was down at Newcastle Marina in Nanaimo. I stopped by early one morning to have a look at the boats that were up on the hard (hauled out of the water for painting and repairs). I was just getting out of my van when a fairly young guy, well over two hundred pounds with a muscle shirt and tattoos, came over and called me an "a-hole." He said, "I know you and you're nothing but a dirty blankety-blank a-hole," so I said, "Look man, I'm not into hurting people but if you don't cut it out I'm gonna let you have it." But he kept it up and came right up to me and gave me a push. I just lost it and tore into him. It only took two good, hard swings and he was on his ass. I ran over top of him and said, "Do you want some more, you son-of-a-bitch?" He said, "No! No!" He got up and as he was going away, his head was turned toward me and he was saying, "I'm going to lay charges against you, you'll see. I'll see you in court." I laughed and said, "Go ahead. You started it and there were no witnesses." (Wouldn't he have looked stupid in court? This biker guy saying, "Your honour, this seventy-eight-year-old man beat up on me.")

It turns out there was a witness. One of the guys off a boat in the marina came up to me a few weeks after the incident and said, "You know, Barrie, I've known you for a few years now to say hello and chat and you always struck me as being a gentle fellow that wouldn't hurt a fly, but I was sitting in my car and I looked over at the boat-yard and there you are beating up on some biker."

Surrey

Anyway, back to the old days. In the spring, I went back to be with my brother Jerry and my mom. By this time

Jerry, Mom and her boyfriend, Ralph Webster, at my grandfather's place in Surrey, where Gramps owned the Dorn Dog School.

Mom had moved out to Wally's Corner in Surrey. She was living at my grand-father Jasper Daniels' place. He'd moved over from Pender Island and had a dog training and boarding kennel called Dorn Dog School. He specialized in Doberman pinschers and had trained one for Bette Davis, the movie actress. Jerry and me used to help around the place, cleaning the kennels and doing odd jobs.

After Mom and Dad split up in 1945, Mom had met a man named Ralph Webster and they were going together. Mom and Ralph had moved in together at Grandfather's place. Ralph had a painting business called Webster Bros Painting and Decorating and he would travel to wherever the work was.

Abbotsford and North Vancouver

The first town we went to was Abbotsford. Ralph rented a house in Clearbrook, just west, and we went to school in the old abandoned wartime airport. I had my own little cabin alongside the house and had it all fixed up with lots of pictures of horses on the walls and little bronze statues of horses. (I was really into horses when I was a kid and I was going to be rancher when I grew up.) I put down red shag carpet and Mom made me nice curtains with horses on them.

My brother Jerry had a bedroom inside the house, but that was fine with me as I really liked my little shack and I could sing my head off in it (I loved singing). We only went to school there till Christmas, then they sent us to a private boarding school on Lonsdale Avenue in North Vancouver. The Kingsley School was run by some English people in a very "Old English" way. If you didn't behave you got the cane, and they called all the kids by their last names. We were Farrell One and Farrell Two. We had to wear the school uniform with the crest on the blazer and a tie, but it was a good school.

This was to be the start of a long series of boarding out with other people during my youth. I didn't realize

Jerry (left) and me in our Kingsley Private School uniforms.

until much later, but it became clear that our mom and Ralph didn't really want us around. Perhaps Ralph wanted Mom all to himself. That's why they kept sending us away. I don't regret it as it didn't hurt me to learn to live with different people and fit in in different circumstances (when in Rome . . .).

Ranching

In the spring we moved to Vernon, but it wasn't long after we got there that Mom and Ralph sent us to live on a guest ranch northeast of Lumby, which is east of Vernon. Three guys who had just gotten out of the army bought this big ranch and were making it into a guest ranch. They were working pretty hard at it, but they weren't really open for business and besides us they only had the odd couple stay there for a while. We stayed all summer and had a ball. We rode horses all we wanted—mostly bareback—got to drive the tractor when they were haying, and swam in the Shuswap River. Being on a ranch suited me just fine, seeing as I had always loved horses and dreamed of being a rancher!

One time they had a rodeo and a boys' steer riding contest, which I went in. I was hanging on to the cinch rope really tight, but I kind of fell forward and was bouncing off the steer's horns. But once I got straightened up I put in a pretty good ride, but I didn't win.

My brother Jerry had a stubborn streak in him. He was usually easygoing, but sometimes he would lose it. When we were in Vernon we both had bikes, and one time we were pushing them when a guy driving a school bus was parking and kind of swerved at Jerry. Jerry stopped and stared at him like, "Go on, I dare you!" The bus driver stared right back and kept coming slowly. Jerry didn't budge and the guy ran right over his bike and then got out and said, "How do you like that?"

Another time, back at the Maple Leaf school, we were all standing up at the blackboard and the teacher had her pointer and was going over some stuff with us. Jerry and me were wearing short pants. Jerry had to take a leak so he

Jerry and I were boarded out for the summer at a guest ranch northeast of Lumby.

put his hand up to ask the teacher. She said no. A short time went by and Jerry put his hand up again, and again the teacher said no. Jerry told her he really had to go, but for the third time the teacher said to wait. Jerry got an angry look on his face—he used to somehow stick his tongue out doubled up and bite down on it when he got mad. Anyway, he looked right at her and just let her all go right there.

In the fall, with school opening getting close, Mom and Ralph started looking for a place for us to board and I guess one of the guys from the ranch knew this old couple way up in the woods behind the ranch who would take us, so we moved in up there. To get to school Jerry and I had to double on the only horse they had, then leave the horse in a lean-to behind an old abandoned school about five miles away and catch the school bus to Lumby (about sixteen miles of gravel road). For a while we had another horse to ride. It was small but a dandy little horse that the ranch loaned us. It looked like a racehorse.

The weather turned very cold and when we'd get back to the horses after school they'd have icicles hanging from their nostrils. When we got off the bus one afternoon, the little horse was dead.

In the long winter evenings, I would do a lot of drawing. I had books full of drawings of bucking horses, trucks hanging over cliffs and a lot of action pictures.

One afternoon when we got back to the farm, Jerry got off and went up to the house while I put the horse away. Afterwards, I was heading up the hill when I remembered I'd forgotten my homework in the barn, so I went back down. It was just about dark and actually dark in the barn. The horse was an old work-horse with monstrous hooves and I made the mistake of walking behind it without talking to it. It cut loose with a hell of a kick, straight out. I must have had my hands in the air because the hoof just clipped my elbow and brushed my chest—another few inches and I would have been a goner.

When I left the barn, I wasn't going to walk behind him again. I went around the front and petted and talked to him like I should have done in the first place.

Kalamalka Lake

In the spring we went back to live with Mom and Ralph. They had moved to Kalamalka Lake, just south of Vernon. It was nice there right next to a nice sandy beach with a confectionery on it and a dock with boats coming in and out. There was lots of swimming and we'd go hiking way back in the cactus and sagebrush-covered hills. In the fall we went to school at the Goldstream school, not too far from the lake. But then in the middle of the term we had to move again, this time to Trail because of Ralph's work.

Trail

Trail was kind of a dreary little mining town (lots of soot from the smelter). It snowed a lot and the snow would always be covered in soot. When Mom would hang clothes out on the line to dry they would get covered with

In 1947, we spent a few months in Trail, because of Ralph's work. It snowed a lot and the snow would always be covered in soot from the smelter.

the stuff. We spent a few months there going to school, but then we moved again, to Aldergrove.

Aldergrove and Langley

We went to school in Aldergrove for a while then I got boarded out on a farm in Langley with an old Scot and his wife. I'm not sure where brother Jerry was at the time. This was in 1947 and I was in the latter part of my thirteenth year. There were lots of chores to do on that farm. They had horses, pigs, chickens, ducks and cows, and the owner was clearing a new field of stumps, roots and rocks. The school in Langley was overcrowded so they had two shifts going and I was on the afternoon shift. I'd get up early in the morning to do feeding, watering and milking chores and then I'd hook up the stone boat to the horse, head out into the new field, load rocks and stumps and take them in to dump them. Then I would quit in time to wash up and head for school. I was like a hired hand, but I wasn't being paid—we were paying them. Something was wrong with that picture. It's a good thing I never minded hard work. I got in a couple of heavy-duty fights at that school, but after the fights we usually became good buddies. That's when I quit fighting.

Edmonton

From Aldergrove we moved to Bonnie Doon in the south part of Edmonton, Alberta. I joined the school football team and had a lot of fun playing. My favourite thing to do was the flying tackle and I also got known as a good street wrestler. I would take on some pretty big guys, sometimes two or three guys my size. I had quit fighting but this was more of a sport.

In the winter there was skating and snowball fighting, and one time Jerry and me built an igloo, but I didn't care for the weather there. In the summer it was deep dust and always a wind to blow it around, and in the fall it was deep

We spent about a year in Edmonton. Here, Jerry and I are ready for school.

mud. Then came the winter and everything froze up with temperatures down to fifty below Fahrenheit. There was thick ice on the inside of the windows and you had to kick the door open every morning. So when Mom sent me back to the coast ahead of her and Jerry to rent a house for the three of us, yahoo!

Back on the Coast

It was so nice to get back to the coast, and even though it was raining lightly it was still green and warm. Of course, the first place I headed to from Vancouver was Pender Harbour to rent a house.

Meanwhile, back in 1945, Dad had met a wonderful lady named Gladys Nightingale, the perfect partner for him. She worked as a secretary for a large firm in Vancouver, but was quite a sailor and wanted her own

Dad made this model of the Wind Song *before he built the real thing.*

sailboat to sail to the South Seas, the same as my dad. This was also the year that we changed our names and Gladys became Sharie Farrell.

Dad had started building his thirty-seven-foot sailboat, *Wind Song*, and together they had finished the boat off in about 1948. He sold our five-acre property in Bargain Harbour to Russ Keillor. (Russ had already bought the property next to us from Tommy Thomas and Dad had let him put up a boat building shop in our lagoon. Russ built quite a few commercial boats there.)

Dad and Sharie were sailing around the coast getting ready for their long trip across the ocean.

When I got to Pender Harbour, I went to see Russ. He had recently moved his shop over to John Daly's in the northeast corner of Garden Bay. John was a good freethinking socialist man with high principles. He

There were three boat sheds in Bargain Harbour at one point. The smallest one was where Dad built Kivi, *the middle one was where he built* Wind Song *and the one on the right belonged to Russ Keillor.*

Top: John Daly's boatyard in Garden Bay. PHOTO COURTESY PIXIE DALY
Bottom: After breaking up with Pixie, John Daly married a lady named Edith Iglauer, a writer and columnist from New York, and she went trolling with him on his boat the More Kelp. *She wrote a book called* Fishing With John *about her experiences.* PHOTO COURTESY HARBOUR PUBLISHING ARCHIVES

was a very good west coast troller and a very humane person. He had a marine ways, which was important for a boat builder, and a machine shop, which helped supplement his fishing income. Russ came along and added a big shed and roof to build boats under cover and his company became Garden Bay Boat Works. Unfortunately, Russ, who was married, was having an affair with John's wife, Pixie, who did the books and also helped out in the shop. In the end, John and Pixie broke up, but Russ stayed married and kept running the business. Later, John married a lady named Edith Iglauer, a writer and columnist from New York, and she went trolling with him on his boat the *More Kelp*. She wrote a book called *Fishing With John* about her experiences. When John died, Edith married Frank White, the father of Howard White, my publisher.

Because Russ owned both his old property and ours, and lived in his original house, our old house was empty. I made a deal to rent it from him starting when Mom arrived. Better than that, he wanted one old shop torn down so I made him a deal to tear down the shop for a couple months' rent.

While I was waiting for Mom and my brother Jerry (I think Ralph either had work to finish up in Edmonton, or he and my mom were split up at the time), I stayed with my friend Neil Newick and his parents.

Mom and Jerry showed up a week later and Jerry and me got busy tearing down Russ's shop. We had fun ripping all the shakes off the roof and swinging around the rafters and tearing stuff apart. Mom was proud of her thirteen-year-old son for making the rent deal on the house, but when the first month was up, Russ gave us our notice. He said he had relations coming that wanted the house, so we finished tearing down the shop and started looking for another place. We never did get anything out of the deal.

We found a place to rent in Madeira Park, just out past the present-day post office. It used to be Spurril's Machine Shop, and a house and the abandoned shop were still there. A guy named Jack Crabb had taken it over, but he'd died recently. It was a nice waterfront property with lots of pencil cedar trees, which are related to juniper and are very fragrant. They're used to line closets because they smell so good and it keeps the moths away.

Jerry and me went to school at the old Maple Leaf school at Donley Landing again. I was working weekends out at Joe Baker's sawmill. He lived at the mouth of Bargain Harbour and had a sawmill with big circular saw blades, and he also built a few boats. He arrived at Bargain Harbour with a forty-five-foot schooner named *Canadian Voyager* that he'd built in Vancouver. The Warnocks and Reg Spicer also had sawmills in the area. I would walk over from our house to Bargain Harbour and Joe would pick me up. But I wanted a little rowboat to get over to work and also to go exploring with, so I drew up a little design and decided to build it. I didn't have any tools, so I looked in the old machine shop and scrounged up an old hammer with one claw, a rusty handsaw that would hardly cut butter and a rusty block plane, and that's what I built the boat with. Joe had given me some clear, edge-grained, three-eighths-inch cedar and the boat turned out pretty nice. It was eight feet long and I had put a varnished plank on the side of the hull at the top and red cedar varnished decks with yellow cedar strips in it. It had varnished oak trim and cedar seats. All the boats I built had alternate red and yellow cedar plank decks, and the decks, trim and seats were all varnished. I wanted them to be attractive and classy looking.

I used that boat for a few months then a guy on a visiting yacht wanted to buy it, so I let him have it for ten dollars. That wasn't a lot of money, but it was okay. That was the start of Farrell Boats.

Before that I had always dreamed of having horses and being a rancher, but that got forgotten when I started building boats. I quit school partly through grade seven and went logging for a while as a whistlepunk, relaying signals between the guys setting chokers and the person operating the yarding machine, for Art Duncan at Middlepoint. I also built a fourteen-foot rowboat in my spare time.

2

The Working Life Begins

My mom and Ralph got back together and the four of us moved to Parksville. Mom had bought a little twelve-foot boat with a one-and-a-half horsepower Lauson engine in it and I brought it across the Gulf to Vancouver Island—just me and my pet crow. (Yes, I had a pet crow for a while.) The little boat only had about seven inches of freeboard. I got as far as Squitty Bay on the south end of Lasqueti Island and spent the night sleeping under the stars. I started out early and got to French Creek by about one o'clock. My grandfather, who had sold the property in Surrey and now lived in Parksville, had a nice property on the Englishman River just down the road from the house Ralph had rented, and he came and picked me up.

Ralph had a job in Port Alberni, working at the pulp mill (you did whatever job you could get to survive in those days) and he had been over to see Bill Osborne, who owned Alberni Shipyard. They were building a lot of wooden fishboats and tugboats. Bill was the brother of Robert Osborne, founder of Osborne Propellers in North Vancouver. Ralph told him about me (I was fifteen years old at the time) and I went over and had an interview with him. He said he didn't really need any more people but Ralph had really praised me so he said he'd put me on trial for a week to

In 1949, the four of us moved over to Parksville on Vancouver Island. Here I am working on the twenty-three-foot plywood boat I built in the backyard on weekends and evenings while working at Alberni Shipyards.

see how good I was. After the week was up, he kept me on. Apprentices were getting fifty cents an hour but he started me at sixty.

He had me laying decking, spilling planks and applying them. This was the same work the shipwrights were doing and his shop rate was twelve dollars an hour, so he was making a good profit on me.

Ralph and me had to walk about four miles from our rental house into town to catch a ride with a logger named Ernie Brown. Ernie was a real character and he kept us in stitches all the way. Then we had to walk another mile or so once we got dropped off in Port Alberni. The drive alone was forty-five minutes.

I built a shed at home where I worked at night and on weekends. I built my own table saw and a twenty-three-foot plywood pleasure boat hull in my spare time, and when I got a week's holiday I built five pram dinghies and sold them all within a week.

I stayed at Alberni Shipyard for ten months then I got work in a woodcraft shop close to home. We made doors, windows and some furniture. While I was there I came up with a method of making little flat-bottom model boats very quickly. They were eight inches long and I did it all with the band saw and a sander. I could make eight boats and cabins in one hour (seven and a half minutes per boat) then I would set them all on paper in the paint room, squirt a dab of glue on each one, pop the cabins on and spray them with varnish all at the same time. Then the owner's wife would stick some decals on them. They sold in all the stores up and down the island.

I quit there after about six months and went to work for Ron Cummins Building Supply in Parksville. Ron also took on jobs doing house renovations and he used to take me out to a house. We'd unload the tools and material and he'd say, "Okay, put up this tile ceiling and lay this oak floor," or "Build kitchen cabinets here," and then he would take off. Sometimes the owners would come by while I was busy working and singing away and they would have big frowns on their faces. I guess the boss had arranged to meet them there because, about the same time, Ron would show up. One time the couple went out to meet him and I heard them say. "What's that kid doing in there working by himself?" and I heard Ron say, "Don't worry, that kid knows what he's doing."

Shipwrecked

I quit there after four or five months and decided to go back over to Pender Harbour and start doing boat repairs on my own. I was going to take the little low-freeboard boat back across the gulf. The morning I left French Creek it was so calm you could see your reflection in the water, but by the time I got halfway across, the southeast wind was coming up, and by the time I got almost to Sangster Island, it was blowing a hard southeast gale and the waves were coming over the stern. Bailing like heck, I headed for the windward beach on Sangster, and I made it without sinking, but just. I grabbed my tools and sleeping bag, got them up to shore and ran back down with a crescent wrench to get the coupling bolts undone and then just ripped the engine off the engine beds. I had been towing a nice little ten-foot carvel-built rowboat I'd built and pulled it up on the highest logs above the high tide mark. There were some dilapidated old hand trollers' shacks there with hardly any roofs left, but they would keep some of the wind off. It had started to rain by this time, but with the help of some gas from the tank on the motor, I managed to get a fire going with my last match then went looking around the island for something to eat but there was nothing. I thought there would be some clams, oysters, berries or something. I roamed the island till dark, then went back, stoked up the fire and crawled into my wet sleeping bag.

Although it was wet, it wasn't too bad. I caught a bit of shut-eye but the southeast howled all night and when I went down to the beach in the morning, there was my new carvel rowboat all smashed to heck. The extreme tide from the heavy southeast must have been just high enough to move the logs around.

Stuck on the island for five days, I roamed around singing songs, looking for something to eat. It kept raining hard so at least I had water to drink. The southeaster finally died at the end of the fifth day. Just after dark I saw a boat off the island, going slow and circling around. It was a gillnetter deciding whether to make a set or not, so I got my flashlight and sent him an SOS. He came in and got his bow up to the rocks and I jumped aboard. He had decided not to make a set as the northwester was coming, so away we went back to French Creek. He had just cooked up a big pot of spuds and he said go ahead, so I ate the whole potful—then three cans of beans and a couple of cans of peaches. He had his car at the creek and gave me a ride home. Mom was real happy to see me as she didn't know if I'd survived the storm or not.

Back in Pender

I caught the CPR boat to Vancouver and then went on up to Pender, where I stayed with my logger friend Neil Newick and his folks again. I got Walt Higgins (he was the big guy I had some fights with at school) to take me back over to Sangster Island to pick up my tools and stuff, but when I got there it was all gone.

Neil Newick, Benny Dubois and me used to chum around the harbour together. Benny bought a new BSA motorcycle and we would all use it. One time I was tearing along full speed on the gravel road in Kleindale and a big black dog came running out chasing me. Somehow he got his head under the front wheel and I upended. I didn't break anything but my legs got badly scraped up and full of little rocks. You could probably have heard my bellowing for miles (not using nice language). The dog probably learned his lesson.

Another time Neil was riding the bike and he was following pretty close behind a pickup truck when a car passed going the other direction and the people in it yelled out a hello. Neil was busy waving at them and not looking ahead when the truck stopped. Neil smashed into it and ended up in the box of the truck.

One time Benny was riding along on the bike and was passing a side road. Meanwhile, a guy was coming down the side road hill trying to start his old truck by letting out the clutch. Right when he got to the main road, as Benny was going by, the truck started. It nailed Ben and smashed his ankle pretty bad. So much for motorcycle riding.

Starting in 1950, when I was sixteen, I did repairs on fishboats at the different floats around the harbour. I only had a little dingy to get around in and not much in the line of tools. I would build new timbered bulwarks on trollers, chopping them out with a hatchet. It was hard back in those days, no mini grinders and such to fair things with.

I built a seventeen-foot boat for Neil's mom. It was quite a little boat. It was carvel-planked with bent oak ribs but hard chines. She didn't have the money for an engine, so it sat idle for a year or so. Then when she had the money, I built a cabin on it. Malcolm Duncan, whose dad was logger Art Duncan who I had worked for, ended up with it and commercial fished it for a few years. Then I built a fifteen-foot plywood boat for Len Larson. Len came from Stuart Island, at the mouth of Bute Inlet, and bought a property in Madeira Park where he gradually built a lodge resort and cabins by himself. That is now part of a housing development called Madeira Park Estates. I worked for Len for a while, blowtorching the paint off and repainting his troller. I'd also go to Warnock's sawmill with him and help load and unload lumber he'd had sawn from beach-combed logs. He built the lodge and all the cabins from that beachcombed lumber.

For a while, I went logging up at Frank White's camp in Green Bay on Nelson Island. (Frank White was 101 years old as I was writing this and he had just published a couple of popular books about his life.) While at the camp, my buddy Neil Newick had a classic barrel-backed speedboat and we would ride back and forth between Pender Harbour and the camp on weekends.

Meanwhile, Ralph and Mom had moved down to Saanichton, just south of Sidney on Vancouver Island, and Ralph was working at a shipyard in Victoria. I took a trip over to visit them and while there I built myself a ten-foot rowboat so I could row over to James

Island, up to Sidney and then over to Sidney Spit on Sidney Island. It was a long day of rowing. I got home late at night but it was a good adventure and I just did it for fun.

My brother Jerry showed up while I was at Mom and Ralph's and stayed for a while. Again I had my own little cabin to sleep in, so we dragged in another cot for Jerry. We got along super well and used to do a lot of wrestling. Sometimes we'd wrestle for hours till we were so exhausted that we couldn't stand up and we'd go crawling to the house laughing our heads off. Mom came home when we were going at it and she said, "My goodness, you guys. The way you go at it the neighbours might think you're really fighting and call the police."

Kyuquot

I worked as a handyman at the Loran radio navigation station on Spring Island, just off Kyuquot Inlet on the west coast of Vancouver Island. It entailed a lot of different things like painting, carpentry, clearing land, running a little work boat, unloading drums of diesel off the Coast Guard ship *Estevan* that was anchored out, then rolling the drums up the long, long dock and standing them up. Another chore I had with the work boat was taking carpenters out to a big rock where they were building a new lighthouse. The swells are always pretty big out there, so I had to get in just as the swell was coming up and then holler "jump quick" and get the boat back out quickly. The carpenters were old guys with heavy toolboxes, so it was pretty hard. With the

For a while, I worked at the Loran station on Spring Island, near Kyuquot.

noise of the engine and the waves, I had to shout really loud and sometimes it would take three or four tries. I'd get pissed off and throw in the odd cuss word and they would get mad at me. They didn't like this young kid shouting at them. It wasn't much fun, but just part of the job.

Back then I used to play guitar and sing and I had lots of time to get a good tan. There were a couple of nice girls there and we became good friends. When the boss found out what I could do with wood he got me to build some new doors for the buildings around there. It was a good summer job. When I flew out of Kyuquot it was on an old rickety bi-plane. It looked ancient. The wind was blowing pretty hard and the wings were flopping up and down. It acted more like a bird than a plane.

Deckhanding on *Swell*

I rested up for a few days then went into Victoria and got a job with Victoria Tug, deckhanding on an old eighty-foot coal-burning tug named *Swell*. The company was good to work for. The tug is still going and still named *Swell*, although she's lately been rebuilt as a charter fishing yacht and doesn't look quite the same, but they did a nice job on her.

We used to work six hours on watch and six off and we would chalk up a day off for every two days we worked. The deckhands had to go down below and shovel the coal bunkers full twice a day. We used to tow barges, sometimes rock barges, sometimes coal, and we would fill the tug's coal bunkers at Nanaimo or Union Bay while we were picking up the coal barges. We would tow the rock barges from the quarry at Blubber Bay on Texada Island.

Brother Jerry (left) visiting me after he returned from one of his deep-sea trips. At the time, Mom, Ralph and I were living in Saanichton, near Victoria.

One time we towed a rock barge down to Seattle and up into Lake Union. When we got there we went out for a night on the town. We hit a few taverns where we were drinking beer and muscatel wine mixed together and we all got pretty drunk. When we got back to the boat, the mate and the engineer got into a fight. The mate, who was known for scrapping, laid an awful beating on the guy and wouldn't stop, so the skipper grabbed a big steel hook that weighed two or three pounds and smacked him over the head and knocked him out. The next morning, everything was okay again.

Towboating on the *A.G. Garish*

It was fun working on the *Swell*, but after about nine months I quit and bought a nice 1939 Dodge car and right away I took a trip up to Clearwater where my buddy Neil Newick was working planting trees. It was easy to

The 1939 Dodge that I bought when I quit working on the tugboat Swell.

get a driver's licence in those days, but I hadn't driven much, so I was a little shaky going through Vancouver.

After that I went up to Pender Harbour for a little while and did a bit of boat work. Then Jerry came along after just getting off a freighter and we went to Vancouver together and shipped out on a big old oil-fired steam tug called the *A.G. Garish*. She was actually a deep-sea tug with the heavy towing gear aboard. The stern was about ten feet off the water and we were towing flat booms up and down the inside waters of BC, so we had to use a ladder to get down on the boom, and that was pretty haywire. She was an awful boat to work on so we only stayed a couple of months.

3

Building Boats

It was 1953 and I was now nineteen years old. After getting off the *Garish*, I went up to visit my dad at Blind Bay on Nelson Island, just north of Pender Harbour. Dad and Sharie had been back for a while from their sailing trip to Hawaii and Fiji, where they sold the *Wind Song*. They had a really bad trip after leaving Hawaii for Tahiti and after fifty-seven days bucking into storms, they ended up in Fiji. That was the end of the offshore sailing idea—at least for a while.

They had spent some time at Sharie's parents' place in Vancouver and while there Dad built a fifteen-foot open boat with a Wisconsin engine in it and headed up the coast looking for property. They bought a nice place behind Kelly (used to be called Granite) Island, just outside Blind Bay. They put in a great big garden and built a boat shed and a cedar pole house with cedar shakes, like our old house in Bargain Harbour.

While I was staying with them, I designed a twenty-four-foot cod boat and decided to build it and go commercial fishing. I made a half model, built a shop and steam box and so on. I fell a fir tree to chop the keel out of, beachcombed some logs and took them to a nearby sawmill to get cut up into lumber, then I got started building. I was doing it the hard way just like Dad did: all by hand (no power tools) and using rough lumber (not a uniform thickness).

I had a nice yellow cedar timber for the stem and it took quite a few days to shape it. It took a lot of chopping, smoothing and chiselling the rabbit line in it. The timber was about fifteen feet longer than it had to be and

In 1959, I moved up to Nelson Island with my dad and Sharie. Here I am chopping out the stern timber with a double-bitted axe on Sea Song, *the twenty-four-foot cod fishing boat I designed and built by hand at the age of nineteen.*

I left the extra length on while I shaped it. When it was finished, I cut it off at the right length and damned if there wasn't a big pocket of rot in it going right down into the stem, so I had to throw it away and start over again—this time with a hunk of fir. Shit happens.

We had some good times there. A lot of sailboat people would stop in on their way north and in the evenings we would have a big bonfire and a wiener roast with some wine, play guitar, sing songs, tell stories and swim.

We had the pleasure of a couple of visits from the legendary Judd Johnstone, the big mountain man originally from Princess Louisa Inlet. He was living in Blind Bay at the time. His dad, Charles "Daddy" Johnstone, would send Judd and his brother Steve high up into the snowy plateau above the inlet for weeks at a time without jackets and shoes and with only salt, matches, a jackknife and a rifle. They would explore miles into the interior of BC. Anyway, he really impressed me. Such a big, jolly, positive man who had nothing bad to say about anyone. To him everything was good and he was a good storyteller.

My pal Neil Newick visiting me while I was building Sea Song.

It took me seven months to complete the

hull (without a cabin) and by that time I was out of my savings and pogey [unemployment insurance] so I got a job logging in Cockburn Bay on Nelson Island for Art Marshall. My job there was hooking up chokers behind a Caterpillar skidder and that earned me enough money to get my boat finished. I had a small party and the next day we launched my boat and Dad towed me down to the bay, where I anchored it. There were a couple of small bunkhouses in the camp and I had one to myself while the cat skinner (the skidder driver) and the fallers had the other.

I was out of money and Art didn't give advances, so it was tough. There was no cookhouse so we were responsible for feeding ourselves. It was hard going for the first couple of weeks, but the guys there were hunters and they gave me deer meat and there was a bag of flour in the cupboard that had been left, so I lived on hotcakes and deer meat for two weeks till payday.

I started building the cabin on my boat at anchor, but it was pretty hard going. Luckily, there was a guy named George Bradshaw, who lived next to the camp, and he came out to my boat and offered to let me put it in his boat shed to build the cabin. I said, "Really?" and of course, I accepted. George had about a forty-five-foot boat he kept in the boat shed. He used it as a store boat and would head north in spring selling to all the fishermen, logging camps, fish buyers and people up the coast, then he'd take the winters off. This was back in the 1950s when the coast was more alive. His boat was a beauty, with a varnished cabin and all and it was so

Sea Song, *before I built the cabin on her.*

very good of him to take it out with winter coming and leave it in the rain, snow and freezing weather so that I could have my boat in there. I got busy at nights and on weekends building the cabin. By then I had named her *Sea Song*.

There was a guy, Jack Edmonds, working in camp who had his thirty-four-foot cod boat *Hazel H* anchored out in the bay and he was going to get a new cabin built on it and replace his engine. I made him a deal to build a new cabin on his boat in trade for his old engine which was a good-running, two-cylinder Vivian.

I did all the work by hand and when the days got short, I used to pack the battery from the camp crummy down to the shed. I only had this tiny little 12-volt bulb to work by. I can't remember how the hell I got that heavy engine out of Jack's boat and into mine, but I got it installed. Over the winter I built both cabins, so I quit logging and was going to tow Jack's boat down to Pender Harbour for him.

Sea Song, *complete with cabin.*

It was getting late in the day and I really should have waited until the next day, but being young and anxious to get to Pender, away I went. When I hauled up the anchor on Jack's boat I noticed that the chain was awfully short and I didn't find out till later that a guy had loaned Jack an extra length of chain so he'd have enough, but Jack and him had a pretty bad fist fight, so without telling anybody the guy took his anchor chain back and threw the anchor in without enough chain on it. I towed the boat to near the mouth of the bay and anchored it as I was going to whip around the corner to see Dad for a minute. I figured it would be okay as it was calm, but while I was away, the wind had come up. It was dark and the boat was gone. I didn't have a good spotlight. It was a black night and the wind had started to howl. I searched and searched for the longest time, but no luck. It seemed hopeless and I was cold and tired, so I finally gave up and headed through the storm to Pender. The boat was found a few days later up at McRae Cove, about eight

The new cabin I built on the old Hazel H *in exchange for the two-cylinder Vivian I put in* Sea Song. *The* Hazel H *was lost, and because I felt responsible I ended up giving Sea Song to the owner.*

miles north, near Saltery Bay, smashed up pretty bad. Somebody salvaged it and towed it to Pender.

Pender Harbour Again

Jack's boat was hauled up on the ways at Garden Bay and I went and had a look at it. It looked like too big a job to repair it and I was just sick. I'd been partying with my buddies for a few days and was pretty hungover and didn't have the will I should have. I felt responsible and figured the right thing to do was to give Jack my new boat.

Back in the harbour, I boarded at the Newick place and took on some repair work. I also did some finishing inside Jack's new boat.

Ralph and Mom bought a thirty-eight-foot pleasure boat, *Lady May*, and were living on it. It was a good boat with a 110-hp Chrysler. Ralph got a job at the logging camp at St. Vincent Bay, not too far away, renovating a house. He needed another man, so I went to work with him up there and we stayed on their boat.

When that job was over, I rented a shop on the beach at Art Duncan's place in Madeira Park and built a room in the corner of the shop to live in. I had it fixed up pretty good, kind of like a boat with a table, bunk and cupboards.

I first built cabins on a few boats that were about eighteen feet long. Then I got a contract to build a

In 1954, Ralph and Mom bought a thirty-eight-foot pleasure boat, Lady May, *and lived on it in Pender Harbour.*

nineteen-foot commuter boat for a logger, Lew Milligan from Vanguard Bay on Nelson Island, with the stipulation that it had to be in the water and running in six weeks. I still had to make a trip to Vancouver to get the materials for the job, so I borrowed a truck from Olsen Brothers Logging (they were logging up Sechelt Inlet and kept their truck at Egmont) and off I went. I got back in a day or so and started flying at it. I had to put in some long days but I got it done in time, doing the woodwork and hard stuff in the daytime and the painting at night. Sometimes I'd still be painting at three in the morning. Lew named the boat *White Wing*.

I took on a job rebuilding a thirty-five-foot fishboat that had been burned almost to the waterline. The job was for Jimmy Wray, a hand logger from the well-known Wray family from Irvines Landing. I was to stay with his family while working on it.

We pulled the boat up next to a shop with a deck coming out to where the boat was, then we jacked the boat up above high water and I got busy getting rid of the burned stuff. What a dirty job it was. I built a plywood roof over it, but the southeast winds howled into that corner of the bay and tried to blow it away, so I had to install guy lines to hold it down. It was a pretty cold place to work, especially in the winter, but I got it finished, in the water and running.

Then my pal Harry Brown and I got jobs logging with a logger named Tommy Gee, who was contracting for another logger, Henry Harris, up the mountains behind Kleindale. Tommy was a real character to work for. He

I built the nineteen-foot commuter boat, White Wing, *for logger Lew Milligan from Vanguard Bay on Nelson Island. He stipulated that it had to be built in six weeks—which it was.* BOTTOM *PHOTO COURTESY DOUG MILLIGAN*

had a good sense of humour and was always laughing and joking around. Harry and I got along good. The worse the name we could think of to call each other, the better it was.

Harry was chasing at the pile (unhooking chokers from logs when they were brought into the spar tree) and I had to settle for the only job left—whistlepunk.

One day we were logging away and Tommy got in the bight of the haulback and broke a couple of ribs. We were just finishing up that setting and had to top the spar tree for the next setting, but Tommy said we'd have to take a few weeks off while he healed up. We didn't want to lose time from work so I offered to top the tree. Tommy kind of laughed and said, "Ha, ha, the whistlepunk is going to top the tree?" Although I'd never had a set of spurs on, I figured I could do it and I finally talked him into letting me have a go at it. It was scheduled for two days after that. I was a little nervous because it was a big tree, about five and a half feet at the butt and had big thick limbs that started low. I'd never had a set of spurs on before, but away I went. Tommy was being a bit spiteful and wouldn't tell me anything—like how to undercut the limbs. If you didn't, the limb would rip some of the tree away with it and tear at your rope. It was all done with an axe. Anyway, to shorten this up, I did it in five and a half hours. Tommy didn't tell me where to top the tree and when I decided I'd better do it, it was about fifteen feet above where we ended up hanging the tree plates [which support the guy lines and pulleys]. When the top was gone, he shouted up, "Do you want to climb down or do you want to hang the pass block and ride down?" (The pass block is the first pulley hung and it is used to pull up the rest of the rigging.) I said, "For Christ's sake, send up that pass block," and after I hung it, I rode the line back down to the bottom. We'd only yarded in a few turns when the top fifteen feet snapped right off at the guy lines and just about creamed old Harry. Luckily, he was fast and there were a few logs there to protect him.

Right after I'd finished Jimmy Wray's boat, I had rented a little cabin from Bill Pieper. He owned the Irvines Landing hotel, post office, gas dock and store. One of his employees was a fellow named Al Lloyd, who came to Pender Harbour and eventually started his own store, Lloyds, which became John Henry's marina and store.

Bill was kind enough to let me use one of his shops, where I built a few small boats in my spare time while logging with Tommy. I built a couple of fourteen-foot plywood outboard-powered boats for the Department of Fisheries, and a fifteen-footer for a salesman from Vancouver.

Irvines Landing was a pretty neat place back then in the latter part of 1950s. Besides the hotel and store, there was lots of nice grassy property to wander around in or play ball or whatever. The Irvines Landing school (now called the Sarah Wray Hall) used to have their sports day or May Day in the field there.

Eunice Fincham, who ran the hotel, bought a couple of nice little ten-foot clinker boats to rent out, so Harry Brown and I rented one by the month to go across the harbour to catch a ride at Madeira Park. One afternoon, after work, we got into a few beer on the way home and took a shortcut under the pier, wide open, and hit a piling dead centre. Well, it sprung that poor little boat from one end to the other and it was never the same. It leaked like a sieve. I felt bad about it and after a while I took it to my shop and re-nailed it.

One night while I was working late in my shop, I looked out and the sky was all red. I looked over to where my little cabin stood and it was burning down. Apparently the oil stove had flooded and started the fire. So I moved in with the Brown family at Lee Bay and boarded with them. Their place was known as The White House. They were a good family, the older ones looked after the younger ones (there were eleven kids) and the mother, Irene, was such a wonderful lady.

When the logging contract was over, Harry and I got jobs at Layton and Webb Logging in Hidden Basin, just inside Billings Bay on Nelson Island. By the way, Rod Webb's son, Roddie Webb, now owns a trucking business in Pender Harbour. Harry and I were up to our old tricks, calling each other vulgar names, and the hooker (the boss logger in the woods) said to one of the guys, "Either those guys are awful bad enemies or awful good friends." Poor old Harry got into playing poker there and when the logging was finished, he left the camp broke.

One morning, when I was boarding with Harold and Evelyn Klein (Harold was one of Norman Klein's sons and the family had a small logging operation), who lived in Kleindale where the Stonewater Motel is now,

Watercolour painting "The White House," by my dad, Mel Daniels,
before he changed his name to Allen Farrell. COURTESY LINDA MATTIS

I got a call from a Pender logger and mechanic named Rocky York. He was a good bullshitter. (His son ended up in prison. He was out hiking one day with his .22 rifle and he stopped at old lady Flynn's house, at the Irvines Landing end of Hotel Lake where the Lakeside Motel and Campground is now, asked her for a glass of water and shot her.) Anyway, Rocky wanted some caulking done on his boat, so I got right down there. His boat was up on the ways at Johnny Haddock's Coho Marina. (His son, Ab Haddock, is still around Pender Harbour.) Johnny had a marine ways, and some floats out past the present-day post office. Johnny told me that it was imperative that the boat be off the ways by 6:00 p.m. the next day because he had a big Chris-Craft pleasure boat coming up.

I started reefing the caulking out of the seams and I could see right away that the seams were shot and the caulking would have gone right through. I told Rocky we would have to put some new planks in, so I stayed under the boat and kept reefing the cotton and cutting out the bad planks while he rushed to get some cedar planking material. The seams were bad in the whole boat, so I just kept reefing. It's a good thing that he brought back some extra material because I ended up putting in seven new planks and recaulking the whole boat. It was a thirty-foot fishboat. I stayed under the boat and worked straight through while Rocky and his wife brought me food and water. I worked all day, all night and all the next day till six o'clock without stopping, working above my head. And I experienced something I hadn't before. About one in the morning I was dragging ass a bit and I guess it was nerves cutting in, but I got a second wind and had new energy, and it happened again about daylight. Six o'clock in the evening came and I had just finished the cementing and painting. Rocky asked how much he owed me. I thought for a minute and said, "Fifty-seven dollars," and that's exactly what he paid me. I always was ridiculously gentle when it came to charging—or maybe just stupid. The job was worth more like a couple hundred dollars.

I went to Madeira Park and rented a shop from Wilf Harper. He was another logger and he had a gravel truck and some other equipment. Some people called him "Haywire Harper." His shop was in the old Spurril's machine shop by the current post office, where I'd lived when I was a kid. I worked out of it for a while and also boarded there. He had a bunkhouse and a bunch of us young guys jungled up in it and ate in the main house.

The first job I got there was putting a new bottom in a new twenty-three-foot water taxi (sounds funny, eh?). Well, there was this fairly young man in Secret Cove who had just got out of the navy and he designed and built this twenty-three-footer to run from Secret Cove to Thormanby Island, a distance of two or three miles. But he designed the boat with about three inches of hogg in the bottom. (Hogg is where the hull, instead of being convex or straight, is concave from front to back.) He thought this would keep the bow down. On the trial run he pushed the throttle ahead and she dove under the water—tried to become a sub. So, he brought it to me to fix, and the only way was to put a whole new bottom in her, so I turned her upside down and got cracking. I

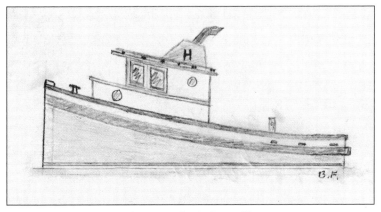

Drawing of the twenty-foot tug I built for Wilf Harper in 1957.

took all the plywood off the bottom, added to the ribs to make the hull straight and put a new bottom on her. The guy later became a naval architect, but I don't think he was a natural.

The next project was putting a new cabin on a twenty-footer. Then I designed and built a little twenty-foot tugboat for my landlord, Wilf Harper. He wanted it heavily built to work around log booms. I had Billy Brown working with me on that one. Billy became a top-notch all-round woodworker and house builder and raised a family of six (three boys and three girls). Billy was Harry Brown's brother and one of the Brown family that I'd boarded with at The White House. Harry was my pal who I'd worked with as a logger many years ago.

The Great Lakes
My brother Jerry had just got off a freighter from a trip to Germany and he came to visit. We had a good time for a few days and he decided that him and I should head back

to the Great Lakes and ship out on a freighter together. (There are lots of big freighters on the Great Lakes.) We went to Vancouver and hooked up with a couple of seamen Jerry knew who were heading back there in their car. The trip wasn't without incident. A couple of breakdowns and hitting a deer, among other things. It was a few days before we got to ship out so we had a fun time on that good Lakehead beer (Thunder Bay).

The freighter we shipped out on was only a little grain freighter named *Star Bell*. It was fun working on the lakes. We would go through the locks into different lakes, from Lake Superior to Lake Huron to Lake Michigan and back to Lake Erie to Lake Ontario. We'd get a night to see the sights in Milwaukee, Buffalo, Chicago, Detroit, Toronto, Duluth and so on. I was hired on as a day man, working eight hours a day and Jerry was a quartermaster.

In my berth on the grain freighter on the Great Lakes.

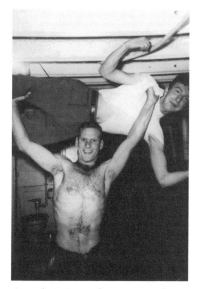

Jerry hoisting a shipmate to the deckhead on the Great Lakes.

The screen door to the officer's mess was no good and they had a bit of a workshop aboard with some lumber and some screen, so I got busy and built them a real good screen door and they were so thankful, they said, "Aha, no more mosquitoes and flies." They wanted to promote me to a winch man, but I said no thanks, I'm just here for a holiday.

Jerry got off at Kingston after a month and a half or so and shipped out on a deep-sea freighter. When payday came, no matter where you were, in port or out at sea, the captain would call you up to the wheelhouse and pay you in cash. I stayed another month or so, then flew back to Vancouver where I bought a car and then went back up to Pender.

Boat Building at Silver Sands

I went back to board at the Harpers but didn't get any work right until Roy "Hoot" Gibson came along. He wanted me to go into partnership with him and build boats in his big basement at Silver Sands, just south of Pender Harbour, and live with them, so I did. He had moved to the area and started a logging company and built a big house at Silver Sands. I remember it had a huge round window like a porthole. Roy had a lovely wife, Bertha, and two nice adopted kids, June and Lance. It was good living with them.

Roy knew a couple of guys who wanted fourteen-foot runabouts. I came up with the idea of building them from plywood without any ribs, just a bulkhead where the seat went and some fore and aft battens on the bottom for rigidity. I just figured that with plywood, you didn't need all those ribs and battens of a typical planked boat. I was the first person around to do this, and I built half a dozen of them. I also built an eighteen-foot cabin cruiser with a wraparound windshield and a wraparound windshield on the cabin top. The top windshield was so you could stand in the cockpit and look over the cabin top.

We built a little pleasure boat for Roy Doyle, a logger from Halfmoon Bay, which is between Sechelt and Pender Harbour, and on the day of the launching there were quite a few people on the float watching to see how she performed. When we untied, Roy pushed the throttle ahead as far as it would go and she just went about a quarter speed with the bow sticking up in the air. He did a couple of circles with it that way. It looked like a failure and there was an old guy there who started to laugh. He was laughing so hard, slapping his knees, laughing at our alleged misfortune. I couldn't help but think how mean-spirited he was. Anyway, it was just some button on the controls was sticking and as soon as Roy pushed it in, she opened right up and went along beautifully at thirty-five knots. I'm not going to say who the old guy was, but he was well known around there and his grandkids are friends of mine. It would just hurt their feelings to know.

While I was at Roy's, some people came to Silver Sands on a boat that they were staying on, the *Calypso*. While they were there, the dad, Bill Copping Sr., was building a big shop to play around in. They lived in New Westminster, and he was a car salesman in town. They were pretty well off. Bill had a nice wife and two kids, Billy and Lois. (Billy now owns South Coast Ford in Sechelt.) Anyway, I helped Bill Sr. build the shop and he paid me well.

While I was at Roy Gibson's, my mom, Betty, died at the age of forty-two. They weren't sure what she died of. She lived a good clean life. Part of it was kidney problems and she had bad headaches for a couple of years before she died. Nowadays, they could probably have found the problem and saved her.

Roy was a good guy, but he wasn't a boat builder, so I was supporting the whole scene there and it wasn't working out. So I left.

Scrap Metal Salvaging

I had an old one-ton flatbed International truck at the time. It was pea green and had "Green Hornet" written on the doors. I decided to go scrounging for scrap metal: aluminum, copper and any kind of junk I could get money for. Jimmy Wray got me started on the idea. He didn't make a business of it, but I did. He was hand logging at Green Bay on Nelson Island and sometimes I'd get a ride up with him and his crew in their boat, take some twenty-litre pails and spend the whole day up at Frank White's abandoned logging camp, where I worked when I was younger. I had a big sledge hammer and I would smash up all the cast iron I could find and have a big fire going to burn the insulation off the copper wire. I would make several trips down the hill loaded down with stuff. Some trips I would have the twenty-litre pails as full of cast iron as I could and still pack them. I'd have a rope around me towing an engine block. I'd be at about a thirty-degree angle just digging in and grunting. I sure used to put the old body through it. When I would take my stuff to Vancouver on the old Black Ball ferry *Kahloke*, instead of sitting up in the lounge relaxing, I'd be out on my flatbed stripping copper wire with a knife.

Malibu Club

Next I took a job at the Malibu Club, up near the mouth of Princess Louisa Inlet. It was originally a luxury resort for the rich and famous, but was now a youth camp. It's one of the most beautiful steep-sided fiords in the world and has a spectacular waterfall known as Chatterbox Falls. I was doing maintenance work, rebuilding walkways, railings, foundations and I also built a new cabin for Malibu's thirty-four-foot pleasure boat. I built it in a shop and installed it on the boat later. I got my stepdad, Ralph—who was now widowed—a job there, and my old buddy Alan Moberg—who I first met when he was living in Pender Harbour, and who was to become a good friend as well as a well-known folk and country musician—came to work there also. After

I left, Ralph stayed on for quite a long time and became quite involved. Malibu was run by a Christian group called Young Life and my friend Don Prittie managed the transportation for them. (Don went on to become chairman of the board of the Greater Victoria Harbour Authority and then general manager of the Canoe Cove Marina group on Vancouver Island.) Don's group had a 126-foot passenger ship called *Malibu Princess* and they would bring in a new bunch of kids from Vancouver every week and take the others out. The *Malibu Princess* was built for them in 1966 and is still running passengers and freight back and forth to the camp.

Towboating Again

After Malibu, I went to work for Doug Fielding in Pender Harbour. Doug owned Texada Towing and he had a few tugboats including some new steel ones (*Scotch Fir, Texada Fir, Black Fir*) and a barge (*Blue Duck*) and he did log towing and such in the area. I was working on and sometimes running a little tug called *Red Wing*. I lived on the tug and we were tied up at Doug's float in Dingman Bay near Irvines Landing. When Doug came back from Vancouver late one night, he was pretty drunk and I guess he didn't want to go into the house, so he came down to the boat and told me to run up to St. Vincent Bay and wake him up when we got there. It was light when we arrived. I called Doug and he got up, rubbing his eyes and looking out the back window. He said, "Where's the barge?" He hadn't told me to pick up the barge in Pender and bring it up, so it was a wasted trip.

Bella Coola and the Mid-Coast

At that time, my brother Jerry was skippering a sixty-five-foot ex-seine boat, the *Bentinck Chief,* that was being used for a camp tender at a logging camp in South Bentinck Arm, just south of Bella Coola on the mid-coast. The boat needed some extensive repairs done and he wanted me to go up and do the job. It was a chance to make some good money, so I sold the old Green Hornet and bought a little better truck from Pender fisherman Malcolm Duncan. I gathered my tools and took a partner with me—Croft Emery Faircrest. He'd come to Pender as a tourist and got into partying and I got to know him. Croft wasn't as fancy as his name. Actually, he was a pretty rugged guy.

We headed out to drive to Bella Coola and stopped to spend the night at his dad's place in Aldergrove, east of Vancouver. The next day we built a plywood canopy on my truck, loaded up a big bandsaw and some other great power tools he had. We got a forty-five-gallon drum and went to the bulk fuel plant and filled it up with his dad's farm status card, so it was pretty cheap. Then we headed out.

By the time we hit Williams Lake, about halfway to Bella Coola, we were tired, just about broke, no gas, no spare tire and we needed a beer. While we were having a beer, we met an old character from what he called "Risky Crick" (Riske Creek, just southwest of Williams Lake) and he invited us to share his room with him. In the morning we got a job for the day loading a boxcar full of lumber. The lumber was 2x12s, eighteen feet long, soaking wet and we had to hand bomb them in. We got enough money to get a room, a spare tire and enough gas to make it. Then we headed out again.

At Anahim Lake, about halfway between Williams Lake and Bella Coola, the pub was a welcome sight as we were dying of thirst. When we left there it was starting to get dark and we found out the headlights wouldn't work, but we had to be in Bella Coola in the morning. So, one of us would lie on the hood with a big flashlight while the other drove. The road had been rough since we left Williams Lake and it had been a long dry spell. The dirt road was packed solid with big rocks sticking up and in between potholes with sharp edges. Then we would hit places where it was deep dust and when we passed a car, we would have to pull over and wait for the dust to settle. It was a pretty rugged trip. When we got there, Jerry was waiting, so we loaded up all the equipment from the truck to the boat and we both slept on the way to the camp.

It was good to see Jerry and his wife, Sundi Stroshein (more about her later), and there were a few other guys we knew from Pender. It was a pretty big camp and the name of the head push there was Viv Williams. He was a meticulous man with plenty of rules and regulations— too many for some—and he scolded us a few times for not doing little things his way. It was a good job and the weather held, which is something for that country in the fall.

When we could get away and go to Bella Coola, we would visit my old logging buddy Tommy Gee and have a few drinks with him. We worked there for more than two months and, when we left, we caught the old *Northland Prince* down to Vancouver. The springs on my truck were ruined from the rough trip to Bella Coola, so I sold it before leaving. The *Northland Prince* operated on a weekly passenger and freight schedule between Vancouver and Prince Rupert. My partner, Croft, had kept the books and he knew how to charge, so we ended up with a pretty good stake. When I got to Vancouver, the first thing I did was go to Brown Bros. Ford to buy a new truck, and then I headed back up to Pender.

Pender Harbour Again

Back in the mid-1950s, when I was still building my boat *Sea Song* (the boat I ended up giving away), I had the engine in but no cabin yet. I had some stuff that needed to be welded up, so I ran her down from Nelson Island to Pender and put her up on the beach at Dusenbury Island in Gerrans Bay, where Roy Dusenbury had a machine shop where he did a lot of welding and engine and prop repairs. He worked a few hours and charged me hardly anything. I thought to myself, what a nice man. Someday I'll do him a favour. So when I got back from South Bentinck, I went to see Roy. By this time, he had sold the island and taken over the Shell garage on Garden Bay Road in Kleindale (which is now the Flying Anvil Studio). It had this big automobile showroom that he wasn't using, so I said to him, "Roy, I know you love speedboats so if you buy the material, I'll donate the labour and build you one." He was happy about that, so I got a bunch of material and got started. I moved into a little cabin behind the garage and it took all winter to build Roy's boat, so by the time I was finished, I was out of money. I guess if you have a big heart, you don't need a big wallet. Roy was really happy with his new boat. She was seventeen feet and he named her *Sea Fun*. She had a big V8 engine and she went to beat hell. Many years later, the motor was shot and Roy's son Dennis got her and made an outboard boat of it. Poor boat. Having an outboard hanging off the back of this fancy speedboat simply didn't suit it.

Just after I finished Roy's boat, Olsen Brothers Logging came to me and ordered a twenty-foot commuter boat for

I built this seventeen-foot V-8 powered boat, Sea Fun, *for Roy Dusenbury. He'd been so good to me, I only charged him for the cost of materials.*

their camp up Jervis Inlet, so I got going on that. They wanted her built with plywood and fibreglassed over, with an inboard-outboard for power. She was a good solid boat with a varnished cabin and she looked pretty good.

A few years later a logger named Loy Haase was running the boat on the way back to camp. The crew had been drinking and they hit a sheer rock cliff at full throttle. The boat went straight up in the air and she hit awfully hard—so hard that when Loy's weight hit the solid three-quarter-inch-thick oak dashboard that went the full width of the boat, it broke in half, but it didn't do a lot of damage to the hull. It smashed in the bow where she hit, but didn't sink the boat.

After the accident, I had her up at Roy's garage outside, upside down to make it easy to work on. Ray and Doris Phillips (Ray's written a couple of books about the area recently) lived close by and their little boy used to play in the yard. He was a cute little guy called Wilf, and I nicknamed him "Wilfred Bone." He'd come over looking for "naaers" (nails) to drive. One day I'd been using black Sikiflex caulking—or maybe it was 5200—on something and I guess he must have stepped in it then got inside the cabin and was walking all over the white ceiling tile, tracking black caulking all over. I think he got just about every ceiling tile.

After I finished building the Olsen Brothers boat, Joe Mickleberry, a young new local guy, came along with a picture of a futuristic-looking fifteen-foot boat with big fins and a step in the bottom. He asked me if I could build it and I said sure. Then he asked me if I would do it, and I said sure, so I did. It was plywood with an outboard. It was out of a *Popular Mechanics* magazine.

I built a few more small boats in the showroom then I met Philis Wise. She was a half-sister to Nels and Pete Hansen, who were loggers, and she was visiting from Cowichan Lake on Vancouver Island. She became my girlfriend and we rented a house on Norman Klein's property at the head of Gunboat Bay. Norman and his two sons, Harold and Gordie, were logging in the hills behind Kleindale. Norm had a big shop out over the water, and it went dry at low tide. He said I could use it, so I did some boat work in it.

That reminds me of a story involving Gordie Klein. One Halloween we were having a big fireworks display at Madeira Park and Gordie decided to help with lighting the fireworks. Somehow good old accident-prone Gordie managed to set the whole works going, and there was rockets flying everywhere and people running and ducking for cover. The pile of fireworks was right next to where all the cars were parked, so a lot of the cars got scorched. Poor old Gord wasn't too popular that night.

Another Halloween, a Kleindale logger, Darrell Harris, brought a whole case of dynamite down to the school field in Madeira Park. A bunch of us took it out to the middle of the school grounds and set the whole thing off at once. It was one hell of a big firecracker and it blew a giant hole in the ground and shattered some windows in the school. Afterwards, we got a couple of shovels out of Darrell's truck, and it took us about an hour to fill the hole back in.

In the early 1960s, Vic Gooldrup came to Pender Harbour from Bella Coola, where he was logging and building big sleds for yarding logs. They were called "donkeys." He built a thirty-four-foot plywood fishboat in Bella Coola and came to Pender with it and started building boats. He was another natural and kept busy at it. He built a house up behind the hospital in Garden Bay with a shop adjoining it. He built some fairly big boats there, one a forty-footer for a young Pender Harbour fisherman, Eddie Reid.

Vic came to me and offered me top dollar to come and work with him, and, as things were a little slow, I went. I worked for him days and then worked at my shop nights and weekends.

Vic was building boats, usually out of plywood. They were mostly water taxis, fishboats and pleasure boats,

Jimmy Reid built the thirty-four-foot gillnetter Hazel Mae *for himself and I built the cabin in my spare time while working for Vic Gooldrup. Harry Brown bought it later and fished it for many years.*

but then we built a thirty-four-foot, glass-over-plywood beachcombing boat for local log salvager, Sam Lamont. He named her *Vulture* and she had round bilges with bent ribs. It was to be heavily fibreglassed for strength so we got a fibreglass expert up from Vancouver for a couple of days to show us the tricks, and we took it from there. In those days, we used liquid MEK mixed with a white cobalt paste to catalyze the resin. He showed us the right mixing, how to wet it out, how many layers of mat and roving to lay at one time and how to get the air bubbles out. We got our fibreglass supplies from a company called Hallcraft Fiberglass on Boundary Road in Vancouver.

Vic then built a steel tugboat and I built a plywood cabin for it on nights and weekends at home. I was also building an eighteen-foot classic speedboat—the kind with extenuated flare and tumblehome aft like some of the old Chris-Crafts—for Norman Klein's son, Harold, at Vic's shop.

I quit working at Vic's and went back to working out of the shop at the Kleins'. There was a tidal grid against the shop where you put large boats up at high tide and then when the tide went out, you could work on the bottom of them. I put a few fishboats up to work on. One was Cecil Reid's (Sonny Reid's dad) and I put in new bulkheads and did some caulking. On Norman Brown's boat I refinished the interior in Honduras mahogany. I also built a nice little sixteen-footer for Dick Wise (my girlfriend Phyllis's brother). It had a little open back cabin and we put a Wisconsin thirty-two-horsepower V4 air-cooled engine in her and she did about fifteen knots.

A guy had his twenty-two-foot Bell Buoy fiberglass pleasure boat moored at the float at the shop and he wanted a fibreglass canopy built for it. I took on the job, but because it was freezing weather, I moved the job into the half of the house that wasn't being used. There was an airtight wood heater in there so I could keep warm and the fibreglass would cure properly.

It was quite a job as I had to build a wooden plug first, lay up heavy fibreglass, sand and fair it and then cello-finish and paint it. Cello-finishing involves stretching Cellophane tight over the part and taping it down with masking tape. You keep wiping it with a damp cloth so it stretches and gets really tight. You then make a slice in the Cellophane where a special cello-finishing resin can be poured in through a bag-like funnel. Then it's a matter of using a printer's roller to spread the resin. When it sets up and the Cellophane is removed, it's so shiny you can see your reflection—and have a shave if you want to.

It amounted to a lot of money, so I figured if I charged him half of what it came to, he should be okay with it. But when I gave him the bill, he said he didn't have the money and said the bill was too much. Time went by and he came to Klein's a couple of times and told me he'd have the money soon. I had already installed the canopy on his boat, so there wasn't much I could do about it. Then he came by one day and was really friendly. He said he'd have the money for me tomorrow. He then said, "I'm just going to take my buddy here for a little spin in the bay and I'll be right back, then maybe we could go for lunch and have a beer." So, I went and unlocked the chain I had on the boat. It was all BS and I never saw the guy again. It was a pretty dirty trick, plus I was broke at the time.

Phyllis and I split up, and Frank and Marge Campbell (Marge was a sister of Norm Klein) rented the house we were in on the Klein property and let me board with them. Phyllis moved to Vancouver and I went to visit her a couple of times. Then she got a job at Ocean Falls, way upcoast, in the cafeteria at the pulp mill. I flew up to spend Christmas with her. I ran out of money while there and had to get a job in the mill to earn enough to get home. I was working on the broke beater, which meant sorting things out when there was a break in the big paper rolls.

Back in Pender, Frank and Marge moved to a little shack at the mouth of Oyster Bay Road, off Garden Bay Road, so I ended up moving in and boarding with Norm and Gladys Klein.

The Campbells wanted a house built adjoining their shack at Oyster Bay, so I took on the job. I built them a good 1,500-square-foot home.

That spring, Phyllis and I got back together and rented a house at Irvines Landing. It was a waterfront property in the northeast corner of the bay. It was the house where fisherman Cecil Reid and his family lived for a long time.

I started working at Garden Bay Boat Works. It was owned by Denny Harling, a mechanic from Vancouver. He'd taken over from Bud Insley, who had it after Russ Keillor and John Daly parted ways. I used to commute by boat, using the fifteen-footer with its eighteen-horsepower Johnson outboard that the Kleins had loaned me.

I worked there for a year or two and built a few new cabins on boats, but a lot of the work I did was out under boats on the ways putting in new planks and recaulking old tubs with bad seams where it was hard to keep the caulking from going through. It wasn't much fun, so I quit.

Fred Crosby had a dilapidated shed to build boats in on the beach in Whiskey Slough. The shed was open on all sides. He was building reasonably priced fishboats, and was a fast worker. At the time, he was building a salmon troller and had another one on order and needed a hand, so I went and worked with him.

I was still living at Irvines Landing and doing small boat repairs in my spare time in the shop that Bill Pieper let me use. This was where I'd been when I built a couple of cabins for eighteen-footers in the shop and put them on the boats later.

First Thirty-two-footer

In about 1965, I decided to build a thirty-two-foot gill-netter, so Bill Pieper let me build a shop out over the water on posts and I drew up a set of plans for the boat. Phyllis and I went up to visit my dad at Green Bay on Nelson Island, where he was building his new thirty-nine-foot sailboat, *Native Girl*, on the shore. I showed him the plans and he said, "She looks good, but maybe you should knock six inches off the height of the hull." So I did, and she came out perfect.

One time while I still had the old flat-bottom boat with the eighteen-horsepower outboard the Kleins had

Keray, Dad and me (left to right) getting together on Nelson Island in 1966.

loaned me, I went up to Blind Bay where Dick Wise was working on Doug Fielding's booming grounds. I wanted a nice, clear log to get sawn up into boat lumber. One kind of got loose just at dusk and I hooked onto it and towed it to Pender. It was a beautiful old-growth fir. I towed all night with that old worn-out Johnson, and the log made beautiful boat lumber.

I went to Vancouver and bought the material for the thirty-two-footer. I got oak for the chines and keelson, where I wanted it extra strong, and yellow cedar for battens. My idea was to keep the boat as light as possible to get maximum speed out of it and make it fuel-efficient. I built her upside down with the decks first, then the bulkheads, chines and keelson. It had 2x10 oak engine stringers that ran the full length of the boat. Next I planked her with one-quarter-inch plywood on the sides and three-eighths on the bottom. At the bow flare,

I glued one-quarter-inch strips of plywood with bevelled edges. Then I fibreglassed her using two layers of matt (glass fibres pressed into a flat mat) and one of roving (glass fibres woven into a fabric—stronger than matt). I was working full time on her, trying to get it finished so I could go gillnetting. A fisherman friend of mine, who fished for the Francis Millerd fishing company (which had a cannery in West Vancouver and buyers along the coast), was going to go to them and vouch for me and arrange for an engine and net through the company, but he procrastinated too long. By the time I found he hadn't done anything, it was too late for the season and I had spent all my money on material.

Then, Henry Whittaker, who had a fishing resort and rental cabins in Farrington Cove on the north side of the harbour, came along and wanted to buy it as a fishing charter boat for his resort. So I finished it off for him. We put a V6-53 GM diesel in her and she did twenty-eight knots dead racked (with the governor off). Henry named her *Klyuhk*.

I knew Mac Macdonald from Princess Louisa Inlet quite well. He owned much of the land at the head of the inlet and was responsible for having the area set aside as a provincial marine park. He was another real well-known character. I had the use of Whittaker's boat for a few days—I think I was finishing up on a few things—so I went over to Madeira Park and picked up Mac and we went on a little cruise to Bargain Harbour, Secret Cove, Thormanby Island and back. It was a good trip and he filled me in on a lot of the history that I wasn't aware of.

He spent his summers in Princess Louisa, at Chatterbox Falls, and his winters in Mexico.

Next, Bud Kammerle, a well-known local fisherman, ordered a thirty-four-foot gillnetter from me. I used the same plan for the thirty-four as the thirty-two (same beam).

Before I started Bud's boat, I built myself a sixteen-foot outboard boat and bought a new forty-horsepower Evinrude from Harold Clay. He had bought a place called B and M Resort, which he renamed Madeira Marina. It was in Madeira Park and had a ways, marina, repair shop and a few old trailers for rent. The boat had a dark purplish-blue hull with lime green interior hull sides, simulated teak decks and floors and varnished mahogany

Me and stepmom, Sharie, at the 1966 launch of the thirty-two-foot Klyuhk *from my Irvines Landing shop. It was the largest boat I had built and it was to be a fishing charter boat for Henry Whittaker's resort in Farrington Cove. The boat is still in Pender Harbour, owned by Randy Edwardson and since renamed the* Gotta Go.

bulwarks. I had cello-finished the hull so she came out pretty sleek. A year later I took a mould off her and built a few of them.

Anyway, I got cracking on Bud's boat, another all-winter project. I also designed a fibreglass-over-wood, thirty-eight-footer for Sonny Reid, who named her *Instigator*. I was too busy to build it so it was built at Garden Bay Boat Works, which was then owned by Denny Harling. Sonny and Marie Reid are a great couple and they went gillnetting up north with her every year until 2014.

Bud gave me a hand with his boat a bit near the end, and one day I sent him to get a steel bracket made to

I designed the Instigator *for Sonny Reid, but Denny Harling built it as I was too busy.*

support the steering ram. He came back with an overbuilt heavy bracket so I said to him, "Damn it, Bud, that's way too heavy." And he said, "Ah, it's only another sockeye." So I said, "If you keep thinking that way, she'll have a full load of fish before she hits the water."

We launched his boat, *Devil Woman*, in the evening and then the party started. The next day, the engine guys came up from Vancouver to do the start-up and then we went on a trial run. Part of the trial included a trip to the Garden Bay Pub. After we were there for a while, Bud decided to head home, so he jumped on his new boat, opened her up about half throttle and tried to circle around between the floats. But he didn't turn tight enough and went right over the float and halfway through Harry Brown's gill-netter *Hazel Mae*. The funny part to this story is that my good buddy Harry used to come over while I was building Bud's boat and say, "Jesus Skindo, you're building her way too light. She's going to fall apart the first trip out. You're wasting your time. Ha, ha, ha." Anyway, when Bud's boat went over the float, it smashed in the side of Harry's hull, went halfway through the deck, smashed down his mast, stabilizer poles and knocked the table off the wall. Then Sam Lamont, the log salvager, was just coming in and he and a couple of fishermen threw a line around the plywood cabin and yarded *Devil Woman* off the float with Sam's boat *Vulture*, and away Bud went out the bay.

Harry never again mentioned *Devil Woman* not being strong enough. It was kind of a rude way to shut him up. Poor old Harry was looking pretty sad as he'd been laid up for a long time with a broken leg and was just about

Devil Woman *being hauled back off the dock by Sam Lamont's log salvage tug* Vulture.

to start gillnetting for spring salmon the next day. It all worked out okay, though, as I had builder's risk insurance on *Devil Woman* and it covered everything. I hired Harry and his dad, Jimmy, who was a wooden boat builder, to repair the boat.

While this was going on, a funny thing happened. I noticed Al Lloyd, who owned the store in Garden Bay, coming around the trail from his store. He stopped, took one look at the boat on the dock, his hands went to his forehead and he spun around and headed back the way he came.

When Bud would get home from fishing, he would rig up the boat with a bridle and go hand logging with her. The crew would leave a whole lot of slack in the rope then open her wide and when they hit the end of the slack the log would come out of the woods, which is pretty hard on a boat. The boat always had a rough life, but it stood up fine. She was still going strong some forty-odd years later until she hit a sheer rock bluff up Jervis Inlet at full cruising speed. She went straight up the bluff, came down stern first and sank in very deep water. That was the end of poor old *Devil Woman*.

After Bud's boat, Phyllis and I drove down to San Francisco for a holiday. When we got back, I had work to start on right away. Frankie Lee, a well-known Pender fisherman, had bought a couple of clinker-built lifeboats off the old retiring deep-sea tug *Sudbury* and made a sailboat out of one and wanted me to make a gillnetter out of the other one. So I hauled her up into my shop at Irvines Landing and got going on her. I raised her one plank in the bow and tapered it down towards the stern so she would sit proud. I then built a little west coast troller cabin on her. We put in a four-cylinder Kermath gas engine and he named the boat *Barnacle*.

First All-fibreglass Boat

Edwin Reid came along while I was working on Frankie's boat and ordered a thirty-four-foot gillnetter. So after Frankie's, I got started on that. I had the hull built and fibreglassed, but then we had some bad southeast winds and extreme high tides and my shop at Irvines Landing was flooding. So I turned the boat right side up and yanked her out of the shop on one of those high tides.

I took it over to behind the Garden Bay Pub where I had rented the big A-frame shop that Vic Gooldrup had built out of sixty-six-foot boomsticks. Vic finished a lot of fibreglass hulls that were laid up elsewhere (he didn't want to do the layup), mostly forty-footers. Vic was a very talented, hard-working man, but he went bankrupt. He moved away, but continued building. He ended up building a lot of big seine boats and packers in Victoria, Bella Bella and near Campbell River. His son Mike eventually took over the business. Vic's brother-in-law, Les Kearley, owned Pelagic Pacific Industries in Victoria and used to lay up the hulls for Vic.

I got Edwin's hull into the shop, turned upside down again. This time—as I had only done a couple of cello-finished boats before and had a tough and frustrating time with them—I got George Matson, who was a professional cello-finisher from Surrey, to come up and he did the finishing on the hull. I learned some tricks from him that amazed me. I could do cello-finishing okay from then on. After it was finished, I waxed it up and took a mould of it. I'd had enough of all the grinding and filling and sanding that went into finishing the outside of the hull of glass-over-wood construction. With a mould, the boats were all fibreglass and they came out nice and shiny.

I had never built a mould before and there was no one around there to ask, but I managed and it popped off okay. Edwin had been in the shop first thing in the morning and had a look. His hull had kind of disappeared while we were building the mould over it, so he was sure surprised to find it sitting in the middle of the shop, right side up, all white and shiny when he came back about two o'clock. We had pulled the mould off, turned the boat right side up and dragged it to the middle of the shop that morning!

While I was finishing Edwin's boat, the *Alice R*, a fellow from Haines, Alaska, came and ordered the first all-glass hull, so I hired three guys and had them laying up a hull for his boat while I worked on Edwin's. I was too busy to do it myself, so I showed the guys how to do the gelcoat and layup. No one else was building all-fibreglass boats in the harbour, but I was never short of balls and it worked out fine.

I took a mould of Edwin's boat off the deck up to the windows. The way I went about it was kind of stupid, though. I wanted to have textured decks, so I contact-cemented vinyl with a rough texture to it to do the deck and then up the side of the bulwarks and up the cabin to the windows. I waxed it really good and laid up the fibre-glass mould on it, but it stuck and it stuck to the plug really good, which was really bad. I worked for a week or so prying and chiselling off all the fibreglass. It was also a hell of a job getting all the vinyl and contact cement off, and then to sand it all down and refinish it. Then I started all over again. This time I got some rubber with a non-skid pattern on it, glued panels down, waxed it up again and it was a success.

Edwin was a real gentleman to deal with. After we'd settled up the final bill, he gave me a thousand-dollar bonus—and that was forty-nine years ago!

While I was finishing the boat for the guy from Haines, me and a couple of guys laid up two more thirty-four-foot hulls out of the mould and sold one to Art White (who you'll hear more about later), and one to a Japanese fisherman from the Fraser River.

I built this thirty-four-foot glass-over-plywood gillnetter Alice R *for Edwin Reid in 1968.*

I got the boat for Haines almost finished. It was spring and I put it in the water to run it to Queensboro Marine in Surrey to get the mast, drum, rollers and all the aluminum railings put on. I took a friend of mine, Bob Sully, with me on the trip and on the way, she caught fire—something to do with the wiring I think. I didn't have any fire extinguishers on board yet, so couldn't contain the fire, and we had to abandon ship. We were a few miles from shore, a few miles north of Middlepoint, so we had a long swim to shore. I didn't think Bob was going to make it. I let him hold onto my shoulders and towed him the last part of the way. When we got to within a few hundred feet of the beach, a couple of guys came out in a little boat and got us. Then they took us up to their house and gave us a few good stiff shots of whiskey. I guess a bit of hypo-thermia may have set in by that time. Then the police showed up and gave us the third degree. The guys who picked us up were really good fellows and they gave us a ride back to Irvines Landing.

I had builder's risk insurance, so the guy got his money back, and reordered later, when Jack Currie had the moulds, but it was a big disappointment for us.

A few days later, my wife, Phyllis, took her life, which hit me awfully hard.

I didn't have any orders lined up and, with all that had happened, I kind of lost heart in the business. So when Jack Currie, who did a number of different things, was a sort of entrepreneur and a bit of a crook, came along and twisted my arm to sell him the thirty-four-footer moulds, I gave in and sold them to him.

After having some time off and partying too much, I smartened up and went to work for Jack, building the thirty-four-footers in North Vancouver. I helped him lay up the first hull then I finished it for him. It was a troller for his brother Bill. We got a couple of guys who worked at Cal Glass Boats—they were building thirty-foot pleasure boats in North Vancouver—to lay up hulls in the evenings and on weekends. We sold one to Bill Prittie, who owned a car dealership in Langley but lived in West Vancouver, and he built his own pleasure boat cabin on it and made a good job. Bill's son Don, who now runs Canoe Cove Marina in Sidney on Vancouver Island, has one of my forty-footers with a fishboat cabin that's been added on to and he is restoring it. It was in pretty rough shape and the conversion from a fishboat was never finished off properly, but Don's making a good job of it. I recently put some new purple heartwood guards and trim

Bill Prittie finished this thirty-four-footer, Annie Mac, *and built a pleasure boat cabin on her.* PHOTO COURTESY DON PRITTIE

Don Prittie's forty-footer, Deep Bay, *before he started on the restoration.* PHOTO COURTESY DON PRITTIE

on it for him. It's going to take him a few years at the rate he's going—he is very meticulous and he's doing it in his spare time.

We sold another hull to Ron Simpson, a lineman for big hydro projects, and one to Mike Forrest, who came from a long-time Fraser River fishing and towing family, and I also finished one for Mike's brother Ray. The guy from Haines, Alaska, whose boat had caught fire, reordered and I finished up one for him. Then Stan Vestad, from the well-respected wooden boat building family up the Fraser River, ordered one, and I finished it for him.

Stan and me hit it off good and I stayed at their house in Delta for the last month of finishing his *Jan Marie*. One day I was working up on the deck of Stan's boat and I went down the ladder to get something. When I got back, I couldn't find my hammer and I got mad and started cursing and hollering, "Jesus Christ, where'd my goddamn hammer go?" Now, Stan is a big Norwegian guy, known to be a good scrapper. Anyway, he doesn't say anything, just slowly walks over with a grin on his face and hands me my hammer. The next day, a friend of his came over to have a look at the boat and Stan says, "I'd like to you to meet Barrie Farrell. Barrie's a pretty nice guy, but don't ever touch his hammer."

I was pretty well running the shop for Jack and doing all the work, but Jack was raking in the dough. So when Stan and me finished his boat, I quit and went north gillnetting with him for a couple of weeks. When I came back to North Vancouver, I went to see Ron Simpson. He had the thirty-four-foot hull he got from us sitting in

Hanging out with my crew at Irvines Landing when I was building boats in Garden Bay. Bob Fielding (with axe), Johnny Nelson in the background behind the axe, Dick Dusenbury, Gordie Gough and Pete Hansen (left to right).

his backyard, and I took on the job on my own, building the cabin, back deck and command bridge. I built it all out of Honduras mahogany.

It was now 1971 and by this time I had met Kay Douglas, who had left her husband, and she became my second wife. Our time together was to be a rocky road.

Ron finished off the boat himself with a little help from his buddies over a couple of years and made a real good job of her. He named her *Annca*. It had a 3160

Caterpillar diesel in her. Ron separated from his wife and lived on it for a while at Mosquito Creek Marina in North Vancouver. He had the boat for several years and eventually a couple bought her and took her on a freighter to Rarotonga in the South Pacific Cook Islands and started a charter business, which was a real success. It was the early 1980s when they took her down there and she's still at it. They changed the name to *Seafari*. As the couple were getting on in years, they sold the business and he built a model of the boat and wrote a poem for her, which he emailed to me.

> I was brought into this world
> By boat builder, Barrie Farrell,
> Of Vancouver, BC in the year
> 1972. I was Christened *Annca*.
> My heartbeat is a 3160 "Cat"
> Supplied by Finning, also of
> Vancouver, so you can see I am
> Truly Canadian! I've been told
> I'm attractive, as you can see by
> My rounded stern, my bottom's
> Quite unique, and I do have flair!
> I am also thick skinned, so I can
> Take a lot of guff!
> I was adopted by Sharon and Elgin
> Tetachuk, and moved to Rarotonga,
> Cook Islands in 1983. I was then
> Re-Christened *Seafari*. We did a
> Lot of exciting things, such as big

Game fishing, rescues, filming, and
Marine scientific research work, also
As a liberty boat for naval ships.
As my adopted parents were getting
Old, I moved on, but still keep in
Touch. I have a Namesake, who I
Modelled for, so you will remember me
THE WAY I WAS

Other Pender Harbour Boat Builders

There were a lot of good boat builders in Pender Harbour in the 1950s and '60s when I was a young man. I've mentioned some of them already so won't repeat myself here.

The thirty-four-foot Seafari *was shipped to the South Pacific in 1983 and used for charter fishing for many years.*

There was Jack "Jock" Cumming, who was an old-time shipwright who built boats like the *Wander Bird*, a thirty-eight- or forty-foot wooden troller, which he sold to George Larson from Blind Bay, who married one of Judd Johnstone's daughters. Jock worked for Russ Keillor and John Daly in Garden Bay, and then built his own boatyard in Gunboat Bay. His living room was full of old Easthope engines, and he used to play the bagpipes.

I remember when Dad was living aboard one of his boats at the Madeira Park government dock. One night he saw Jock's nephew, Jackie Cumming, get off the bus from Vancouver and come down the float with a new power saw he'd bought. Instead of untying the lines to his boat, he started his power saw and sawed a couple of hunks out of the tie-up timber. I guess he just had to try out his saw and save some time.

When I was just a little guy, there was Dary Carter, who had a marine ways and shop by Canoe Pass where the big Lougheed mansion is today. He was an excellent wooden boat builder and built Cedric Reid's fishboat *Nancy R* and Edwin Reid's first *Alice R*. Both were all-wood gillnetters of about thirty-six feet. He built a lot of bigger boats plus a lot of beautiful clinker rowboats, all varnished. His goal was to build a thousand boats before he died. He moved to Nanaimo and I don't know if he reached his goal. A fellow named Jim Sharp went on to buy Dary's place and build boats there.

Marshall Rae made a lot of twenty-six-foot, clinker-built, pleasure and commuter boats on the south side of Gunboat Bay where Headwater Marina was later located.

Ed Wray from Irvines Landing built a gillnetter called *Little Poacher* as well as a couple of small tugs and a landing barge. Ed was one of the large Wray clan. He later became a big ship captain on the coast, and part owner of the landing barge *Georgia Transporter* with Syd Heal.

Fred Crosby went to work for Russ Keillor while he was still building boats in our lagoon in Bargain Harbour. He also worked with Russ at John Daly's place in Garden Bay. Fred was a natural boat builder. He would get a lot done in a short time and when Russ would leave for a while, he'd get even more done. After Russ left Pender Harbour, Fred went out on his own and built a lot of wooden fishing boats at a shop in Whiskey Slough (Gerrans Bay). He knew what would satisfy fishermen—something basic and functional—and he'd build it fast and at a reasonable price.

Carl Remmem, from the well-known boat building family up the North Arm of the Fraser River, moved to Pender Harbour in the late 1950s and built a few boats there. He was a fine boat builder and his son Ronnie took after him.

Don Penson came to Pender in about 1965 and went to work at Garden Bay Boat Works and also worked for me for a while on Edwin Reid's boat. He went on to open his own shop at the head of Gunboat Bay and built a lot of fast commuter boats. He and Bob Fielding partnered in Garden Bay Marine Services and they built some bigger boats. Don was one of the last builders still going in Pender.

Jimmy Reid, Cedric Reid's son, worked for Vic Gooldrup for a while when I was there and then went on his own. He commercial fished in the summer and built boats all winter at his place, first in Sinclair Bay, then in Whiskey Slough. He built a lot of boats, mostly plywood, but some planked, including a forty-two-foot planked troller. Jimmy was a good friend.

Bert Gooldrup, Vic's brother, who was a fisherman, built a few gillnetters and I think his son Dick took after him.

A few of the local fishermen built their own boats during the winter. In those days, you had to be handy to make a living. When you live in the country, you learn to use your hands and do things. Some of the fishermen—the Mackays for example—built some really nice boats.

My dad built quite a few boats in Bargain Harbour. There was the twenty-four-foot cod boat *Kivi*, then a thirty-six-foot sailboat, *Wind Song*, plus a lot of twelve- to eighteen-footers. He used to build beautiful twelve-foot, easy-rowing double-enders. After he came back from sailing *Wind Song* to Hawaii and Fiji, he went to Vancouver and built a little fifteen-footer with a Wisconsin in it. It was an open boat and, when he bought property on Nelson Island, he converted it into a really neat cod boat. He raised the sides, put a west coast troller cabin on it, put in a lot of ballast and made a live well in the hold. He named it *Gray Gull*. Then he built a thirty-foot sailboat and after that a forty-five-footer. Then, he built his most beautiful sailboat, the thirty-nine-foot

Native Girl. The last one was a forty-foot Chinese junk *China Cloud.* He built over forty boats all by hand on the beach, with no electricity or power tools. There have been two books written about my dad's life and his boats: *Salt On The Wind* by Dan Rubin and *Sailing Back in Time* by Maria Coffey.

There was also some guy, I think his name was Barrie something or other, who built a few boats too.

Yes, back in the good old days, until about the late 1960s, there were boats to build and lots of fishermen catching fish. I don't think there are any boat builders left in Pender Harbour now.

It's a shame what happened to the boat building and fishing industries on the coast. I mostly blame

Dad's beautiful ketch Native Girl, *which he started building in 1965.*

government and their various fishboat buy-back programs, which got rid of so many small boats but kept the big seine boats and draggers. It killed all those small coastal villages that had fleets of gillnetters.

The Haywire Boat

Back in about 1953, Fred Crosby got hold of the *Hazel H*, the old boat of Jack Edmonds. Jack was the guy I gave my twenty-four-foot cod boat to after I lost his boat while towing it. It got smashed up pretty good but Fred rebuilt it. He used it to run around the harbour, then sold it to his brother-in-law, Jimmy Devaney. Now, Jimmy had to be the most haywire man I have ever met, way worse than "Haywire" Harper. My brother Keray, who was in his late teens at the time and had been working building roads, got the boat after Jimmy was through with it and I offered to fix it up for him. I guess Jimmy had wanted to lift the engine and it looked liked he had taken a hammer and bashed about a six-inch hole in the cabin top (it was the new cabin I had built less than a year before) to put a line in to hoist the engine. Then he had driven big spikes partway into the engine beds and wrapped heavy wire over the engine to hold it down. The steering wheel and all the steering blocks were held on by driving dozens of shingle nails partway in and bending them over. He had chiselled all the ribs off where they met the horn timber right from the back bulkhead to the stern post so he could caulk it from the inside, and he'd caulked it with strands of rope and strips of old pants—some still with buttons on. The stern bearing was gone and the shaft had been thrashing around so bad the propeller had chewed into the horn timber about an inch and knocked the heavy gumwood shoe off, so he had nailed a piece of cedar shake on in its place. The whole boat was a disaster and he used it to take his wife and kids, even in bad weather, over to Texada Island. But anyway, Keray and me got at it. I put new ribs in the stern, new varnished red gumwood guards and caps, took the yellow cedar windows down to new wood and varnished and bolted everything solid, put on a proper shoe and painted the whole boat. She looked like a new boat when we were done. Keray renamed her *Wander Boy*. He kept her and lived aboard for quite a while, then sold her to a friend of his, Dave Harding (there was a whole family of Hardings from Blind Bay on Nelson Island). Dave was a good troller and made enough in a few years to order a new forty-foot Wahl troller he named *Freedom*.

Brother Jerry

My brother Jerry left school at an early age—fifteen or sixteen—and shipped out on a deep-sea freighter. He continued working on many different freighters and going all over the world. He grew up quick and had some pretty rough experiences. He told me about coming to in a hospital in Germany all covered in blood and beat-up bad. No wallet or ID and nobody spoke English. He had lots of other scary stories.

When he did decide to come back and work on the coast, he got a job as a quartermaster on the old Black Ball ferry *Kahloke,* running from Horseshoe Bay to

Gibsons, but it wasn't long before he was back on the freighters. When he came back periodically, we would always get together and have fun. One time when Jerry was on the coast here he got a job on a whaling ship, the *Lavallee.* They were out at sea and got their harpoon line caught in the propeller, so the captain asked if someone would volunteer to dive down and cut it out. Jerry volunteered. It was rough weather and the stern of the ship would come right out of the water and come crashing down with a smack, so it was pretty dangerous. Jerry dove down with a knife in his teeth so he could hang on with both hands at first, then he hung on with one hand, grabbed the knife and cut the rope out of the prop. He had to be really careful coming back out. If he swam up when the ship was coming down, he could have got his head split open. When Jerry came in off the ship, he didn't bother to tell anyone what he had done, but our stepdad, Ralph, happened to have a chance meeting in a nightclub with a guy who turned out to be the captain and he told him what Jerry had done.

After Jerry came back from the Great Lakes, and before he went up to South Bentinck Arm, he met Sundi Stroshein. It wasn't long before they got married and had a big wedding in Wilson Creek, just south of Sechelt. I got a kick out of seeing our dad in a suit. It was so out of character to see the old hippie Allen Farrell in a suit.

Jerry and Sundi rented a little house at Davis Bay, which is also just south of Sechelt, and Jerry studied for his 350-ton captain's ticket. It was hard for him with his limited education, but he hung in and got it. He got a job running a fairly big fish packer and he hired brother Keray as one of his deckhands. One day Jerry and Keray were having a wrestling match on deck and Keray's wristwatch got flipped off and went overboard. Quick as a wink, Jerry dove off the high bow of the packer and got the watch before it sank.

Next, Jerry and Sundi ran a fish-buying scow up north for Pender Harbour fish buyer Duncan Cameron. Duncan's whole family was into fishing and, besides fishboats, they owned this fish-buying barge. One fall, after Jerry and Sundi towed the barge back to the harbour, they rented a house from George Robinson. (He was the uncle of famed rock-and-roll DJ Red Robinson.) Over the winter, Jerry continued to look after the barge and buy fish for Dunk. Jerry would take the money home and hide it. One night while they were out, someone broke into the house and stole eight hundred dollars that Jerry had hidden. That was quite a bit of money back in those days. He suspected someone but could never prove it.

When a big tug called *Viking* something or other caught fire on the other side of the harbour, they ran her up on the beach and let her burn there. It was a really bad cold snap, but Jerry would row across the bay at night in the bitter cold with his trusty hacksaw and saw away on the four-and-a-half-inch shaft to get the big brass propeller off. He couldn't get much of a stroke with the little saw but after a full week, he got it off and dragged it down the beach and buried it. Some salvage guys came along a few days after with a little tug and a barge and started salvaging what they could. A couple of days later,

Jerry was having a beer with them in the Garden Bay Pub and he hit it off pretty good with them. He told them what he had done and said, "You guys can have the prop. I don't know how I'd get rid of it anyway." All that work for nothing.

According to publisher Howard White, two or three Viking tugs burned under suspicious circumstances while the company was being wound down by owner Jack Ryall. The hulk in Pender was eventually towed to Green Bay where it can still be seen. Jack lived on Francis Peninsula for many years then moved to Nova Scotia.

Next, Jerry and Sundi rented the apartment above the old store at Irvines Landing and took a little time off to enjoy life. After a while, they went to South Bentinck Arm to run the logging camp tender. After that, they moved to Sechelt and Jerry got a job skippering another little ship out of Vancouver.

One night in 1962, Jerry came home from the boat and there was a party going on at Sundi's Uncle Rubin's place. I don't know what went on there but Jerry left right away and went up to Sundi's parents' house, got a gun and shot himself. He didn't die right away, but crawled a mile or so down a gravel road to where the party was going on. He tapped on the window and said, "Please help me. I've shot myself," but he died on the way to the hospital.

What a sad time. We were so close. He had his 350-ton skipper's ticket and a wife who was a beautiful person in every way, and three little daughters: Bette-lyn, Lenore and Wendy. He was only twenty-six years old. I still miss him a lot and often think of how it might have been.

A few years back, Jerry's daughter Bette-lyn, my brother Keray and me got together, searched out Jerry's grave at the Seaview Cemetery in Gibsons, which had been neglected for years, and planted some flowers on it. Keray suggested we put a ship's steering wheel on his grave, which I thought was a good idea after all the years Jerry had spent behind the wheel on big ships to small ships. I have a nice teak wheel and I have to get busy and build a case for it and probably pour a little cement pad and bolt it down. It made Keray very happy that we were going to do that. I ought to be ashamed of myself; the grave has been neglected for more than fifty years.

Over the years, I became friends with Ron Simpson, the hydro lineman who I built a thirty-four-footer for and whose boat I later worked on in his backyard. Ron had talked to Stan Vestad, the fisherman whose boat I'd finished and gone gillnetting with, about him and me building a big shop on property that Stan had on the Fraser River waterfront in Annieville Slough. The idea was to build it using power poles that Ron could get free, delivered. So we got the poles and got started. Ron borrowed a little excavator and we dug all the holes for the poles and hired a crane to put the poles in the holes. We even used poles for the rafters. Ron was quite a guy for making deals. I never liked bartering myself; somebody always comes out on the short end of the stick, usually me. When I got the crosspieces on the rafters, we started laying the plywood on the roof.

Westport, Washington

About this time, an American, Art White, got in touch with me. He was one of the first customers for my all-fibreglass thirty-four-footer. He'd bought it as a bare hull, without even a cabin. He tracked me down and wanted me to design and build a twenty-seven-foot fishboat for him, and he talked me into going down to Westport, Washington, to do it. So Kay and I headed down there and he supplied a trailer for us to live in. Art was a fisherman and he wanted to start a business building fishing boats using a Farrell hull, and he wanted me to take a mould off the boat. I got started designing and building the boat so it had the proper beam to be easily trailered (eight feet, six inches) and could be made into either a bow picker, where the gillnet is set from the bow, which was common on the Columbia River, or a conventional gillnetter, where the gillnet is set from the stern.

I built the plywood hull, fibreglassed it and cello-finished it. Then I waxed it and laid up a mould off it. Once I got the mould off, I turned the hull right side up and proceeded to finish it. Once I got the cabin and decks built, I installed a 440 Chrysler engine, fuel tanks, steering, net drum and rollers. I also did all the interior finishing—working by myself.

I got all the hydraulics finished and the boat all painted and varnished and then we were ready for the launching and trials. She did good on the trials; we got thirty-five knots out of her. The secret to this and my other designs was keeping the boats light. I also had a slightly unusual but effective design, using a regular entry at the bow and a sort of gull-wing shape on the bottom of the hull. They were doing something like this in England at the time, and I modified it into my design. It made the boat more stable and helped it get up on the plane faster. I also had a big flat section in the middle, about twenty-seven inches wide at the stern and tapering to nothing at the bow.

While I was finishing the first boat, we got a couple of guys in to lay up three hulls out of the mould and I finished two of them as bow pickers and put 440 Chrysler engines and water jet drives in them: a Hamilton in one and a Berkeley in the other. We used jets because the Columbia River, where the boats were going to be fishing, was very shallow. Jet drives work well but they aren't so great when you're packing a load. These two were thirty-five-knot boats also. We sold the other hull to a guy and he had Westport Shipyard finish it up for him. At the time, Westport was building a variety of thirty-four- to thirty-six-foot commercial boats, mostly gillnetters, but now they're building megayachts.

It had taken me seven months to do all this, and I'd been working in the US illegally and got paid in cash, so I took the door panel off my station wagon and stashed my stake in there before crossing the border.

The Farrell Thirty-seven Moulds
When we got back to Canada, Kay and I rented a little cabin in Gunderson Slough, on the Fraser River in Delta. However, there'd been a change of plans about the Vestad property. Our deal was off, but it wasn't Stan's fault. I'm

not sure exactly why it didn't work out. It might have had something to do with the harbour authorities.

I also found out that Mike Forest, the Fraser River fishing and towboating guy who I built a fibreglass thirty-four-footer for when working for Jack Currie in North Vancouver, had given Palmer Boatworks in Maple Ridge permission to flip over the hull I designed and take a mould off it. It wasn't patented so I said, "Ah, to heck with them, I'll just design and build a bigger and better one."

So I did, and I designed a thirty-seven-footer. Palmer went on to build many of the thirty-fours or a lengthened and raised version of it.

It was 1970 or 1971 now and I rented a shop on Gunderson Slough in Delta from Paul Stockland, who was previously a boat builder with his brother, but who worked mainly as a lineman. It was a good, large shop with a big bandsaw and joiner planer, two marine haulout ways (one outside and one inside). The only problem was that it had a big open back, facing out over the river, and in the winter the wind whistled in pretty bad. Anyway, I got started building the plug for the thirty-seven-foot mould. I didn't have any orders when I started and by the time I finished the mould, I had eight orders, with no advertising, just word of mouth. Conditions weren't the best for fibreglassing, especially when I was spraying the gelcoat on the plug to start the mould and the snowflakes were blowing in on me. I'd hired a few guys to help with the layup of the mould and it was freezing weather, so when you washed your hands in acetone, it was mighty

The Avante was a thirty-seven-footer that I lengthened to forty feet by bucking off the stern, setting it up further aft, then filling in between.
PHOTO COURTESY DON PRITTIE

cold and it weeded out the men from the boys. A couple of guys couldn't take it and had to be replaced.

I had a hard time finding good men to work. One young fellow wasn't experienced at anything. A plug would be upside down so the keel was on top, and he would say things like, "That big long thing on the roof of this thing . . ." His name was Dumbrouski and me, with my sense of humour, said to him, "How did you get the Brouski?" and he said, "No, it's Dumbrouski," so I answered, "I know about the Dumb part, was just wondering about the Brouski part," which got a laugh out of everybody. Poor kid. Hope he can take a joke. He's probably doing well.

4

Family Man

On January 15, 1972, my son Allen was born. I was in the delivery room at the time and I got to hold him when he was just a few minutes old. I looked down at him and said, "Hi, little guy," and that nickname stuck with him throughout his younger years. His siblings still call him that sometimes.

Besides being a tease while still in diapers, Allen was quite the climber. The phone was hung quite high on the wall and he used to slide a chair over to it, then pile books on the chair until it was high enough to reach the phone, then climb up and pretend he was phoning.

One time while I was working in the shop, I heard some hollering coming from the house, so I went outside and there's Little Guy, who was still in diapers, halfway up an aluminum extension ladder that was leaning against the shop. It was extended right to the top of the building, which was about twenty-five feet high. I got on the ladder and climbed up behind him and let him keep going right to the top.

Another time he saw us jacking things up with a hydraulic jack and that became his favourite toy. He'd go around jacking up everything and if the jack wouldn't reach, he'd put blocks under it until it did. One time I was sitting at my desk talking to a customer and Allen was behind the desk with me where the customer couldn't see him. Allen had his trusty jack with him and all of a sudden the desk starts going up in the air. I'll never forget the look on the guy's face when he saw the desk levitating.

Farrells in the USA

I got the thirty-seven-foot mould laid up and all the stiffeners on the outside, ready to pull off the plug when Art White, the guy from Westport, came along and wanted a duplicate mould for down in the US, so we made a deal. He would pay the full cost of building the second mould and I would get a 5 percent royalty from each boat. We agreed that neither of us would sell in the other's country.

I had to be really careful lifting the mould off the plug as it wasn't meant to stand up to a second use. After I got my mould pulled, I got a hold of a friend of mine, Ed Rae. Ed had done some fibreglassing for us when I was working for Jack Currie in North Vancouver. I made a deal with Ed to lay up my boats out of the moulds, so he rented a shop and I sent the mould over. I then got Art's mould done and shipped it to him. However, just before I'd finished his mould, he reneged on the royalty agreement and I agreed to settle for $2,500, which was peanuts compared to what I would have got out of the royalties.

The First Thirty-seven Hulls

I brought the first hull over from North Vancouver and built the plug on it for the cabin and foredeck mould, then the back deck and cockpit moulds, as well as the caps, bridge and hatch moulds.

Harry Olson, a Prince Rupert fisherman who was living in Delta, got the first assembled boat, which had only all the moulded parts put together. He took it next door to the Remmem boatyard, which was right alongside my shop, to be finished. The boatyard was run by Harold Remmem, brother to Carl Remmem who built boats in Pender Harbour. Harry put a 3208 Cat diesel in her. Back then—this was about 1972—I could get a 3208 with a Twin Disk gear for $5,300. Now they want $40,000 or so.

The next guy in line was a fisherman named Tom Wilson, and I took a contract to completely finish his boat, as I did with the two boats after his. I was under the gun to get all three finished for fishing season.

I wanted the first one to be a showpiece so I went all out on it and hired Erling Vestad Jr., Stan Vestad's brother, to do the interior finishing and I was going to have teak panelling on the exterior cabin sides. The two boats next on the list were for Egmont fishermen Reg Philips and his son Terry. I had one in the shop alongside Tom's that I was finishing, and the other was outside.

Destroyed by Fire

I had my car in the garage getting repaired for a day or so, so I got a taxi to work early one morning and as we turned down and along the gravel road behind the shop, I was busy talking to the lady taxi driver. All of a sudden she looked past me, pointed and said, "Was that your shop there?" I looked and there was nothing but a black charred mess, still smouldering. I paid her and got out. There were a few guys standing around. John Vic from Vic Enterprises (a major ships chandlery at the time) was one of them and he said to me, "What are you going to do now, Barrie?" and I said, "Well, I still got my hands." So when I got my car back, I started looking for another shop and found one in lower Surrey, west of the Turf Hotel.

My back deck mould was far enough away from the shop that it didn't get burned and the thirty-seven that was outside was half gone. Anyway, I moved what was left over to the other shop and went to a pawnshop to get some tools.

Before the fire, I had a twenty-seven-foot hull shipped up from the US for a customer and I took a mould off it. I pulled the mould off the hull and then the fellow that bought the hull took it down to Dean Garin boat works in Richmond (they were only around for a few years) to be finished and I laid up another hull in the mould. Luckily, I had pulled it out of the mould and delivered it the day before the fire, so I borrowed it back to take another mould as the original one had burned up. So, I had the back deck mould for the thirty-seven in the shop and the twenty-seven hull, and I was laying up a back deck for the thirty-seven and waxing the twenty-seven hull to take a new mould off. I was in Vancouver on business and when I got back to the shop, there was the guy I had borrowed the hull from in my shop loading the hull on a trailer. He had heard a false rumour that everything I owned was going to be seized and wouldn't listen to me. He finished loading the hull and away he went with it. All that time I spent loading it, unloading it, turning it over and putting six coats of wax on it—wasted.

Then, to top things off, the fire marshal came in the next day and said I couldn't fibreglass in the shop because of the fire hazard and because it was a double-occupancy building. Shot down again. So again I went looking for a shop.

I didn't find one, but my friend Aldo Stradiotti from North Arm Transportation found a shop on Bridgeport Road in Richmond. It was a big shop on a half-acre lot and it had a house with a nice upstairs and a good basement suite. The shop was big enough that I could have three thirty-seven-footers in it at once. The rent was $800 a month, with a three-year lease and an option to buy the property for $85,000 at the end of the lease.

But back to the fire. I had insurance on the boats I was building, but none on my own stuff. When it came to collecting from the insurance company, it was a case of no one with a good business head being with me. I had a lousy accountant and nobody to back up my talent. Anyway, I made out a statement for the insurance company and took my accountant with me (I don't know why) for a meeting. He just sat there through the whole meeting and never said a word, and the insurance guy in his big fancy office spent most of the time looking out the window at his great view. It seemed he couldn't have cared less what the settlement amount was. When I made out the bill to them, I only charged them twelve dollars per hour shop rate and took it really easy on the hours with no mark-up on the materials. It ended up that I came out with enough money to repay all but a few thousand dollars, and that had to come out of my pocket. If I'd had more business sense, I could have got twice the money I did, but again, there was no one to advise me and I was too gentle when it came to the accounting. It was a lucky thing that most of my moulds for the thirty-seven were over at Ed Rae's shop for layup.

When I moved to my new shop in Richmond, all three customers with the thirty-sevens that burned reordered. But this time I was wise and stayed away from the finishing. I subcontracted that work to other builders after I had the boats assembled. The problem was that the quality wasn't as good as if I'd have finished them. The guy who took on finishing Tom's boat bragged about being a fourth-generation boat builder and kept repeating how good he was, but he made a real mess of the finishing. He covered everything in the cabin—and I mean everything—with vinyl and just lapped it over. For his oil stove, he built an open-backed box and fibreglassed it to the back of the cabin. When it came to putting the fuel line to the stove, he drilled a hole through the cabin so there was bare plywood between them. He simply put a flange on the inside of the cabin with a tube to the stove, and the fuel had to flow over bare wood between the inside and outside, so naturally the fuel ran down inside the wall. He also put the running lights on the wrong sides, so Tom pretty near got ran over the first night fishing. Anyway, I had to go fix everything. I had taken on finishing a fourth thirty-seven for a Steveston fisherman named Alex Melnychuk and the contract was pretty slim, so I couldn't get anybody to take it, and I had to finish it myself. It tied up part of my shop and took a long time to finish. Alex named it *Atlas Mariner*. Building the kit boats was helping subsidize Alex's boat.

The orders came rolling in and Ed moved his operation from North Vancouver into my shop, so all the moulds were in my yard and nearly all the crew were Ed's men. Ed was building the hulls under contract to me with his own guys and I had a couple of my own guys helping me with the assembly. Ed was a good worker and could get production out of his men. Sometimes he would holler, "Hey, you guys, she's kicking" (when the resin was getting hard, or setting up) and the guys would get their butts in high gear, but the resin wouldn't really be kicking, he just said it to get them going faster.

Ed's crew was a bunch of long-haired, pot-smoking guys and they had a squawky little radio turned up as loud as it would go with that hard rock music. It would just about drive me nuts, but they were good workers and they produced quality work.

Sometimes I would get a phone call in the middle of the night from a fisherman who was up north fishing and wanted to get his order in ahead of his buddy who was going to order one the next day.

Besides putting together boats, I also did all the office work, sales, ordering, payroll and repairing and building moulds at night, but I had an accountant in Langley (not the same one who dealt with the fire insurance) to supposedly check everything over. One day I thought I'd check over my past invoices from Gwill, my fibreglass

Hoisting a thirty-seven-footer out of the mould at the shop in Richmond.

Looking towards the house from the mezzanine of the shop. The boats are all thirty-seven-footers. Note the boat on the far left was being rebuilt after its stern was damaged in the fire.

supplier in Vancouver, and I found they'd made a $500 mistake in their favour. I had it reversed, but the accountant should have been on top of it.

Kit Boats

I always preferred selling kit boats to finishing boats myself, even though I enjoyed finishing. Every boat was so different, with different finishing standards, electronics, appliances and so on that it was very hard to estimate the cost ahead of time. With kit boats, I knew exactly where I stood, how much each part cost and how long it took to put together the pieces. A typical kit boat would consist of all the moulded parts assembled, the motor, shaft, rudder, rudder shoe, windows, hull trim and the visor on the bridge installed. From there, the owners would take the boat away to be finished elsewhere. On occasion, we'd send out the bare boat with only the moulded parts assembled, which was even easier.

By this time we had taken in my wife Kay's five kids. Kay's kids had been living with their father and things weren't going so well. The welfare people were going to separate them and send them to foster homes, so I took them all in so they could be together. I went from being a single man with no worries to a guy with a wife, six kids, and a very demanding and labour-intensive business, so when the stress built up too much sometimes, I would go on a toot for a couple of days to relieve the tension. The kids ended up with me for most of the next ten years or so.

I lengthened a twenty-seven-foot hull to twenty-nine feet, six inches, and took a mould off it and sold two or three of them. They performed good and went fast, but were a little flighty at high speeds, so I took a skill saw and cut the mould right down the stern and up the middle to the stem, which was the only place the mould was still being held together. I grabbed the mould by the ass end, spread her twenty-six inches and then she was a good, stable boat. I built quite a few hulls and eventually built a cabin/foredeck, bridge, and back deck mould for her. She was wide enough now for a thirty-two-footer, so

I lengthened one and took a mould off her and lengthened the cabin and bridge and took moulds off them. I
also made a set of moulds for the thirty-two as a sport
fisher/pleasure boat. So now I was making hulls that were
twenty-seven, twenty-nine-and-a-half, thirty-two and
thirty-seven feet. Even though I'd been taken advantage
of with the royalty agreement with Art White, I sold him
moulds for the twenty-nine-and-a-half-footer and the
thirty-two-footer so he could build them in Westport.
He built a lot of Farrell-design boats under his company
name, Snowball Industries, but he never gave me any
credit for the design or royalties.

To my sadness, Ed Rae and I had a falling out and
he quit on me. It was the summer, so things had slowed
a little. I got a small crew and kept things going for the
summer then hired more men in the fall when things got
flying again.

This was nothing to do with the falling out over the
shop, but Ed wanted me to co-sign for a house he wanted
to buy. I got hold of my accountant and he said I really
didn't have any equity in anything. All I had were all
the hulls that I kept Ed producing, which I paid for as
they were built, but they weren't registered, so they didn't
count. Ed was a little upset at me when I said I couldn't. I
don't think I explained it to him very well.

Ed and a fellow named Ashley James, an egotistical
Australian guy, rented a shop in Richmond and were
doing fibreglass layup there, so Ed and me got together
and made a deal for them to lay up just the hulls in their
shop, which was good for us as it gave us lots more room

in our shop to lay up all the cabins, decks, bridges and all the other parts, and do the hull assembly.

Richmond Building Supply moved in next door to me and there was no fence between us, so I used to joke with them, "Did you know my price on lumber goes down as the sun goes down?" Of course, I would never do that, but I had an old guy staying with us and working for me and he stole a couple of planks one night. Next day I scolded him and made him take them back and apologize.

I had one of Ed's younger brothers, Mickey Rae, working for me. He worked with Ed in my shop before and he knew about fibreglass, but not much about boats. Mickey thought he was just a fibreglass man, but I recognized his potential and took him under my wing. He was easy to get along with and smart and it wasn't long before I had him installing engines and doing the assemblies. Then I made him foreman of the shop. I also got him building moulds. He came up with some great ideas on his own for speeding up production—overhead cranes and wheels on everything, and assembling the cabin, cabin top, bridge and trim all on the floor.

Teaching Mickey and letting him have free rein made him realize his ability, and there was no challenge too great after that. We are good friends to this day. He is living in Texas and is still working. He also has his minister's degree. My nickname for him is "Saint" and he calls me "Foul." (I'm not sure where he came up with that one.) He says those were the most exciting working days of his life.

Another young fellow that worked for me, a guy who I could see was going to go places, was Bob Fielding, who came down from Pender Harbour. He stayed in my lower suite and his girlfriend came down from Pender and stayed with him. He worked right alongside me and one night we were working late and I had two thirty-sevens alongside each other about six feet apart. Bob went to jump from one to the other, slipped, came down full length and smacked his forehead on the cap rail. Shortly after, his head swelled up like a balloon, but he kept working. As I mentioned earlier, Bob went on to partner with Don Penson in Garden Bay Marine Services, where they build boats, docks and had a towing business.

The second year in Richmond, 1974, I turned out fifty (right on the nose) thirty-seven-footers, plus some twenty-nines and thirty-twos. Wow, that Mickey guy! One time he assembled a thirty-seven kit with engine and all the rest of the extras in three and a half days. One day the crew worked around the clock.

I built an extension to lengthen the thirty-seven fish-boat cabin to make it a pleasure boat and I built quite a few of them.

One time when I was building the *Atlas Mariner* for Alex Melnychuk, Ron Simpson, who'd helped with the new shop at the Vestads', was visiting at my shop. Alex wanted to go to Queensboro Marine in Surrey to get a measurement, so Ron offered to give him a ride. It was about a half or three-quarters of an hour drive, depending on traffic. After Alex got his measurement—about eight-foot-something—he held his thumbnail on the tape measure all the way from Queensboro Marine to the shop with the tape all coiled up in the truck. Ron had a hard time not laughing. Sometimes it's just the little things that hit a guy funny.

Another funny one was after I built a boat for a guy, he brought it into my shop the next year to have the fish hold made into slush tanks (instead of ice). I just put three-quarter-inch plywood on either side of the hold, but now the old aluminum pen boards were an inch and a half too long. The owner of the boat, who was a scientist who just fished in the summer, said, "I'll cut the pen boards for you on the bandsaw." I went into the shop a while later and saw that instead of just cutting an inch and a half off one end of each pen board, he was cutting three-quarters of an inch off each end of every board. I couldn't believe it and I just went by and pretended I didn't notice.

During the last year of our lease in Richmond, our older kids used to come out to the shop on weekends and earn a little money doing some fibreglassing or other things like laying up hatch covers. One of the boys, Rusty, would also chip all the fibreglass off the large clamps and oil them up. There were about eighty of them.

As I mentioned, I had a three-year lease with an option to buy the property for $85,000. It was about 1975 now and I was so busy building boats that I left it until almost the end to try to raise the money. I had an acquaintance, Ray Ferris, a former used car salesman who did some business for me once in a while, working on trying to raise it. I don't think he tried very hard.

Anyway, I didn't get the money in time and the place was worth $250,000 at the time and going up fast. It's worth millions now. The reason I didn't have the money on hand to buy the place is that I would only take a small down payment with an order, and then when it was time to start building, I would get half down. Meanwhile, Ed had got ahead of me laying up the hulls and I told him to just keep pumping them out, so I had my yard full of hulls, plus hulls in Ed's yard and also some hulls in DelDon Marine's yard (they were building boats for a few years and used to finish some of my boats). I'd already paid for all those hulls, so I had a lot of money tied up.

Nanoose Bay

I still wanted a place of my own but couldn't afford the Vancouver area. Instead I ended up buying a three-acre piece of property in Nanoose Bay on Vancouver Island. I sent Ray Ferris over to make arrangements to have a new shop built. He started right away and I got a couple of months' extension on the Richmond shop so I could keep up production while the new shop was being built.

I managed to borrow $85,000 from the Industrial Development bank, which was helping small businesses, and I had a $25,000 operating loan at my bank, so I was able to get the land cleared and the shop built quickly.

When Ray offered to go to the island and look after construction of the new shop, he asked me for $800 up front, so I asked him how much he was going to charge me for the whole job, and he said about three grand. We went to the office and I started to make him out a cheque when I got called into the shop, so I just signed it and asked him to finish making it out. He did and then came out in the shop and said, "You're too trusting, Barrie." I had a funny feeling, so later I checked my chequebook and found there was a cheque missing near the back of the book. I took the number down and when I got my returned cheques from the bank, sure enough, there was the cheque made out for $1,000 in somebody else's name. It was in Ray's handwriting and made out on the date he was in my office. I just hung onto the cheque until the final payment to him was due.

Construction of the shop came along fine. We had a good contractor doing the building, but Ray was doing the purchasing and getting a kickback on everything. When it came time for Ray's final payment, he presented me with a bill for $25,000 (a long way from three grand). I showed him the cheque for a thousand dollars he had embezzled and he said just take it off my bill, sort of like, "so you caught me, so what?" I had bought a new flat-deck truck to bring my fibreglass materials, motors, fuel tanks and other stuff over from Richmond, and I ended up giving Ray the truck plus cash. He'd also made enemies for me ahead of time. I went into the building supply store in Parksville and introduced myself. The guy said, "Oh, you own Farrell Boats. In that case, I guess I can quit hating Farrell Boats then." So it was good riddance to Ray Ferris (or so I thought).

My foreman, Mickey Rae, stayed on the mainland and it was quite a move with all the moulds and hulls and so on. It was four or five boat-mover trailer loads. The new shop was a pretty nice concrete block building about the same size as the shop in Richmond. We had a "gala" opening party and my musician buddy, Alan Moberg, came from the mainland to entertain us. I brought the thirty-seven mould into the shop and tipped it up on its side, put plywood down in it and used it for a stage. A lot of people showed up and it was a good party.

A fellow named Dave Wheatley from West Vancouver wrote me a letter asking for employment when he heard I was opening a new shop on the island. I hired him and now he has a successful boat repair shop in Nanaimo. Another fellow, Roy Brown, who'd just finished his boat building apprenticeship in Australia, came to work for me. He now has a successful business, Independent Shipwrights, in Coombs on the Alberni Highway. He has a large boat building and repair shop and has built some fairly large buildings on his property, where he rents out bays to other businesses. His wife, Cynthia, has a good-sized ship's chandlery store there.

Ferris had a company drilling for water out in front of the new shop in Nanoose Bay and they went down 1,200 feet, where they hit salt water, so they stopped and buggered off. I got some diviners and the first two guys were weird: the first guy swung his gold pocket watch back and forth like he was trying to hypnotize us, and the next guy had a stick and did a little dance. The third guy agreed with me that it looked pretty good up in the far corner of the property where there were willow trees, so he tried there with a bent piece of wire, and you could see it bending down when he went over a certain spot. There was a few people watching and I asked him if I could try it. Damned if it didn't work for me. A couple of other people tried it and it didn't work for them, but it did for the lady who tried it last. So, I got the drillers back and we got water at 110 feet.

I brought over quite a few hulls to Nanoose. One of them was a thirty-seven-footer for a fellow named Joe Cox. It was assembled, but he wanted it semi-finished with the interior roughed in and in the water and running. But the financing was taking a long time to come through, so it was on hold. Finally, when it did come through, he phoned and all he said was, "Hi, it's come through. Bye." He was a man of few words.

I bought a new forty-foot double-wide modular home and put it on the back of the property. There was a house in the front of the place, but it wasn't big enough for the family.

Things weren't quite as hectic in the new shop, but I was busy enough. I semi-finished a few and completely finished a thirty-two-footer, all in teak, for a guy called Matt who was a beachcomber in Port Alberni. We put a big V8-71 GM diesel in her. He was one of the only customers I had trouble with. He ordered special things like a 32-volt electrical system and then on completion of the boat, he said he didn't order them and I let him go without paying the complete balance owing—and even then, had trouble collecting. Another thing that happened, which was my fault, was that I had put three-station Morris controls (in the cabin, on the bridge and in the cockpit) but they don't work well if you have too many sharp bends. Anyway, the controls were sticking, so I had to go out to Port Alberni to try to fix them. Matt was beachcombing with her so when the controls would stick at the stern station, he would have to run from there into the controls in the cabin and he would bang his head on the overhang of the cabin on the way in, so he had a few scars on the top of his forehead. The first thing he did when we met was lift up his hat and show me his scars. Me, with my sense of humour, said, "Oh, slow learner, eh?" Well, he didn't think that was the least bit funny. As a matter of fact, he got madder than a hornet. I thought we were going to come to blows.

Anyhow, I got the controls working better, but when it came to collecting the money owning, I had to send one of my more persuasive, heavy friends to get it.

I built a thirty-seven for a father and son in Campbell River. We put a 71 Volvo in and she did twenty-three knots. I semi-finished her (in the water and running). They commercially fished crab with her and named her *Barracuda*. She's now in Pender Harbour being used for sport fishing.

The people from Malibu Camp ordered a thirty-seven-foot open boat for hauling freight and passengers. We put a little Perkins diesel in her and I finished it.

Things were a little less demanding at the time, so I didn't mind semi-finishing some of the boats in Nanoose.

I built myself a twenty-nine-foot, seven-inch (exactly) boat with a 455 Oldsmobile gas engine in her and we named her *Peppy*, after the little dog we had. She was light and fast. I had the drum and radar and everything on her to go gillnetting, but again I was too busy to get out fishing.

Speaking of our little dog Peppy, there was a big Alsatian guard dog next door and Peppy and him would play together for hours and then they would lie down in his doghouse and have a snooze together. One night, I got wakened up in the wee hours to a bunch of yelping and screeching. The big bugger was trying to kill Peppy, so I ran down the hill in my undershorts, through a pond that was frozen over, breaking through the ice, to where they were. I grabbed a hunk of 2x4 and started smacking the brute over the head until he was out. Peppy was pretty chewed up but survived, and when he got better he used to follow me around like there was a string between us. I never did trust Alsatians; they were too unpredictable.

I bought a nice corner lot at Arbutus Park Estates, in Nanoose, had a pad poured and moved the double-wide into it and we all lived there. It was a nicer place to live than on the shop property.

Things were going pretty good and a real estate guy told me that if I wanted to sell the shop, I would probably double my money. But this was the early 1980s and the damn interest rates went sky-high—up to 23 percent—and I was pretty highly mortgaged, so it hit hard. Plus, the orders dried up because no one was going to borrow money to build a boat at that high interest rate. The bank was going to cancel my $25,000 operating loan. I was still dealing with a bank in Richmond (which I'm not supposed to name) and the assistant manager came over for a meeting with me. He said he was interested in becoming a partner in the company because I had a good product and the rates wouldn't stay up forever. I told him that I had a personal cheque for $18,000 because I had just sold a fishing licence that I had taken as part payment on my boat, *Peppy*, that I'd just sold. The assistant manager said, "Oh, just give us the cheque and your operating loan will be safe." I did, and guess what? They cancelled my operating loan anyway, so that pretty well finished me.

I was building a thirty-two gillnet kit boat for a guy in Richmond and he paid me in cash, so I just said to myself, "to heck with the bank," and I kept the money.

After that, I was pretty well shut down for a while, contemplating bankruptcy, but I think they wanted $700 to do that.

New Ownership

I had the property up for sale—just to try and get enough out of it to get out from under it. Then, Don Piccolo, who owned Cal Glass Boats, which was building small fibreglass speedboats in Richmond, came along to talk about taking over the place. I named a very low price for the property and company, but he said he needed another boat building company like he needed a hole in the head. However, he said he was willing to take it over if I stayed and ran the shop. He said, "I'll give you six thousand a month, plus a truck." I took the deal and he was able to scrape up a few orders to get started. But guess what? He hired Ray Ferris to run the office (a bad start). Ferris wouldn't hire any of the good men I had working for me. Instead he hired about a dozen green people. There was a thirty-seven in the shop that was on hold and the guy wanted to go ahead on it, but he wanted the cabin raised so the cabin top would carry through aft at the same height, not a step down. So, I had to build a cabin top from scratch and I was the only one there who could do it.

A bunch of new Cal Glass runabouts with damage to them were shipped over from Richmond for me to repair. Adding to that, I had to try to get production while training a dozen green people and taking orders from Ray, the crooked guy who had screwed me pretty badly. He would come running into the shop and shout things like "The next person who steals a pencil off my desk gets fired," and petty things like that. Don Piccolo treated me pretty good though, but a few months was all I could take. I took a few days off and decided to quit, but before I did, I looked up my former foreman, Mickey Rae, who was living in Comox and had just finished a job. I got him to come down and take over from me so they wouldn't be stuck. Again, Mickey did a great job of running the shop. When I first told Ferris I was going to quit, he said he didn't want me to, and if I did, he'd tell everyone that he had to fire me because I drank too much and that's exactly what he did, even though I got Mickey for them. Cal Glass and the Nanoose shop didn't last much longer before Don Piccolo went bankrupt.

Hard Times

It was kind of a bad time in my life. I had used what money I had to pay some of the bills incurred by the business (small guys first), as all my debts weren't settled when Don took over. My wife, Kay, had left me but I was continuing to look after the kids while she got settled in Vancouver. We were renting a house up towards Bowser and I had taken Bucky Crook's boat (my old *Peppy*) there to finish the interior, so I worked on that.

The two oldest boys went to live in Errington with a woman named Grace Salter. It's a long story, but the two boys were really acting up and social services got involved and placed them in Grace's care. Eventually Kay took the three youngest, including Allen, to Vancouver, so I gave up the house and went to stay with friends of mine, Doug and Florence Watson, for a while. Somehow I lost the double-wide and the Arbutus Park lot, but I did end up with some money out of it and paid some more bills.

After a few weeks, I wanted to see the kids, so I drove over to Vancouver and had a visit. While I was in Vancouver, I went to see a friend of mine, Ralph Rolston, who owned Seair Marine and who had finished quite a few of my boats at his shop in Vancouver's Coal Harbour. He had gone bankrupt and was now renting small premises near his former shop in Coal Harbour. He had bought the moulds for a small ocean-going sailboat, the Vancouver 27, which was a real good little boat. It was designed by Robert Harris with input from my friend George Hartley. Ralph and another fellow were preparing the deck/cabin moulds to take a part out of, but they didn't really know what they were doing. They were applying PVA, a mould-release agent, but hadn't waxed the mould first, which is a no-no—you have to wax first. I never used PVA as it spoils the shine. I always just used wax and had good luck with it. I offered to give them a hand for a few days, and a few years later I was still working for Ralph. We only worked in that shop long enough to do a couple of Vancouver 27 kit boats and then we took on the job of lengthening a Farrell twenty-nine-foot, six-inch named *Fiddlers Green* to a thirty-four. She was originally built with a large cabin with the idea in mind of lengthening her. It was a horrible shop to work in and when it rained hard, the shop flooded. We'd have a couple of big pumps going and I'd be working in hip gumboots. Ralph worked full time as a purchasing agent for the school board, so I worked alone most of the time. He was a great guy to work for. He paid me well, got me a station wagon when my car broke down, put up with my shortcomings graciously—and I did have a few at the time—and helped me out of a few binds.

We moved out of the Coal Harbour shop and rented a pretty big shop on Bewicke Avenue in North Vancouver. The front was on Bewicke and the Mosquito Creek Marina was at the back. The shop was built by Bob Findlay for his boat building operation. His company was called Fibo Boats and he built a lot of gillnetters from a John Brandlmayr design. Bob owned the shop when we rented it, but he was in litigation with the Squamish Indian band. They owned and ran the marina. After about six months, we were renting from the band. Bob was a real character and it's too bad nobody wrote a book about his life. He started out fishing up north when they fished out of open boats with just oars and a sail. Then he was in World War II and was one of the guys who landed at Dieppe. Later on he was building boats and gillnetting and he used to do a lot of poaching. One time while poaching up Indian Arm at night, he spotted a Fisheries patrol boat. Bob shut off all his lights and put wet gunnysacks over the dry exhaust to quiet things down. He was sneaking down the Arm quietly and all was going well until the sacks dried out and caught fire. Then the chase was on. Bob got away because his boat was pretty fast.

Bob had his own airplane for quite a few years and he didn't have a pilot's licence for a long time, but that didn't stop him. One time he was leaving North Vancouver and he was out on the airplane's floats. He gave the prop a spin and away she went, but the throttle was advanced too far and the plane was up on the step almost right away. The wind pressure was holding the door shut and by the time he finally got it open and into the plane, he was right across the harbour and just about to smash into the docks at the Bayshore Inn. He yanked the throttle back just in time. I can't remember them all, but Bob had many, many stories about crash landings and near misses.

When I was building the moulds for my new thirty-four by twelve-foot boat, Bob came to work for me and we became good friends. Bob passed away a year or so ago at the age of ninety-six.

The Vancouver 27 was a good boat and Ralph sold quite a few, mostly kit boats, with the engines and ballast in. I semi-finished a couple and completely finished a couple of others. We were getting the hulls laid up by Steveston Fibreglass and I was laying up the deck/cabin, hatches and all the other parts and doing the assembly. I thought it was kind of funny that two customers in a row had boats built and were both named Cliff and they were both little men. Their last names were Man and Putman.

After a few years things slowed down for Ralph, but before they did, I had a visit at work from Don Mooney from Mooney Enterprises (formerly DelDon Marine), who had finished quite a few of my boats. He said that if things ever slowed down here, he'd like me to come work for him. So, I kept that in mind and when things petered out for Ralph, I went to work for him.

Ralph Rolston, owner of Seair Marine. I built a lot of Vancouver 27 sailboats for Seair.

They were located in Richmond at the north end of Number 6 Road. Don's two sons, Danny and Joey, worked with him, and his wife, Helen, worked in the office. They had about eight to ten men working there.

When I first came to Vancouver after things fell apart in Nanoose, Kay had rented a house on Victoria Drive in East Vancouver and I rented a room in the West End of downtown Vancouver. I used to spend as much time with the kids as I could, but things weren't good there. Kay was partying a lot and away from home and the kids were roaming the streets till all hours of the night. Trying to help with money didn't work, so I talked Kay into getting back together with me for the kids' sake. She had a boyfriend at the time, so it wasn't easy.

I rented a nice four-bedroom apartment in Maplewood Gardens in North Vancouver, east of the Second Narrows Bridge. Things were okay for a few months, but then Kay took off to live with her boyfriend and left me with the three youngest kids, including my son, Allen (the oldest girl, Brenda, was living with Kay's parents in Nova Scotia). Anyway, it was pretty hard being a single parent and commuting to work in Richmond, but we managed and the kids were good.

At Mooney's, a fellow had brought a thirty-eight-foot Gulf Commander hull and cabin in to be finished, but the cabin looked kind of bald, so the first thing I did was to build a nice, rounded overhang all around it with lots of overhang at the front. Then I took a mould off it, thinking we might use it again. However, after a while, I suggested to Don that we sell the mould to Forbes

Cooper, who was laying up the Gulf Commanders at his shop in Port Coquitlam, but Don said no. The owner of the boat had just sold a machine shop in Prince Rupert and he had his own funny ideas. He was putting a big Volvo in and he wanted it in the stern with an outdrive, so I installed the engine and outdrive, but he wanted it moved forward with a large recess in the transom, so that when he tilted the leg up, he could reach through a manhole in the deck to change his propeller. I had to cut a big opening in the transom and bottom, and build a big fibreglass box on the inside. As well, the sides of the cabin were rounded with no thought of how you would install windows in it, so I had to make up special teak frames for the windows. The boat was named *Sea Cott*.

The next one was a fifty-foot Gulf Commander that Cooper had sold as a bare shell to Bob Johnstone from Johnstone Fabricators on East Pender Street. I installed two big GM diesels and made up the struts and rudder patterns, then had them fabricated out of stainless steel and installed them. The next thing I did on her was to cello-finish the whole cabin. After that I did the teak bowsprit and some other finishing. When we launched her, Bob got me down to do some finishing touches on the boat in his boathouse by the Bayshore Inn in Coal Harbour. She was named *Summer Tan*.

While I was working at Mooney's, Don's sons, Joe and Danny, and a bunch of their buddies made plans to do a parachute jump and asked me if I wanted to join them. I was 48 at the time. I said sure. There was sixteen guys that were going to jump, but at the end, only four of us jumped. The day of the jump, I was sick and of course, they said, "Oh, yeah, good excuse for chickening out." Out of the three guys who jumped (Joey, Danny and another guy), the other guy broke his leg landing.

A week later, I took my son, Allen, who was about six years old, and we went out to Abbotsford and did a jump. It was a pretty scary experience, especially as I don't like heights to start with. We were 2,800 feet in this small plane with no door. The other two guys jumped and then it was my turn (what the hell am I doing?). You have to put your left leg out first, and stand on a little step, then swing out and hang off the wing strut until they tell you to let go. Once the chute opened, it was fine.

I was heading out with my son a couple of weeks later to do another jump (it was only twenty bucks to do a jump in those days), but when I told Allen what I was up to, he said "No, you're not!" And I said, "Well, you watched me come down the last time and it was fine." He said, "Oh, yeah, just beginner's luck. If you're going to keep going, let me out of this car right now." So I didn't go and I never did another jump.

Mooney's ran out of boats to build so I went back to work for Ralph in North Vancouver for a while, but he wasn't extra busy. He had moved to Lynnwood Marina, where he was building the occasional Vancouver 27, so when the shop on Bewicke became vacant I rented it.

It was kind of a sad time in my life. I was alone again, except for my son, Allen, and I was partying too much, so I went on the wagon and stayed on for twenty-five years.

I poured a concrete floor in the shop, built a mezzanine floor and put a new roof on. I landed a job building a new cabin and new back decks on a forty-foot crab boat. Once that was done, I got another job lengthening a Carlson gillnetter and putting a new stern on it at the same time—more of a rounded stern, for well-known Pender Harbour fisherman, John Malcolm. His boat was called *Summer Star*. John was a heck of a good guy to work for. When the job was done and all squared up, he gave me an extra thousand dollars, but something went wrong at his bank and the cheque bounced, so when he came to fix it up, he gave me eleven hundred for the trouble.

The 1980s: Building Farrells Again

I hadn't been building my boats for a few years, since things went sour on Vancouver Island. I put a tiny ad in the *Vancouver Sun* newspaper, in the "boats and engines for sale" section saying "Taking orders for Farrell Boats." I got quite a few calls and a commercial fisherman/scientist named Len Fanning came into my shop the next day and said, "How do I order one?"

I said, "Just put five hundred down and I'll put you on the list."

He didn't know that I didn't even have a mould. I figured I would borrow the thirty-two mould from Art White, who had been making the thirty-twos in Westport, but wasn't making them anymore. He drove such a hard bargain—he kind of forgot about the good deal I gave him on the moulds—so I said to heck with him and got a whole bunch of lumber and started building a new mould from scratch. Actually it was a blessing in disguise because I made some improvements and the new thirty-two ended up a lot prettier than the old one.

I've always said I wish I'd have been born thirty years earlier, back when the coast was alive. There were fish canneries, logging camps, homesteads and fish buyers in every little bay up and down the coast. There was lots of fish and the trees were right down to the water's edge, so hand logging was great. The boats were wood, so each time you built a new boat you could improve on it and make it prettier, like the Wahl boats. They weren't too good-looking at first, but then they got prettier and by the time the wooden boat building industry petered out, they were lovely creations. (Ed Wahl and his six sons built them up in Prince Rupert and were probably the most successful wooden fishboat builders on the coast.) The only drawback with building fibreglass boats is that it costs a lot of money to build a mould, so however it comes out, you are stuck with it.

Family Woes

In the meantime, I had some domestic problems. The two older boys had come back to live with Allen, my step-daughters Debbie and Mitzi, and me at the Maplewood Gardens apartment and they caused a lot of trouble around there, picking fights and whatnot, and I ended up getting evicted. They were wild young guys, but they eventually turned out fine. I rented a basement suite in

Surrey, on 132nd Street from an East Indian couple who treated us good and were very nice people. The boys went back to Vancouver Island, so things calmed down a bit. We did fine in Surrey. The kids were good, but eventually the two girls moved on, one to live with a friend and her family and the other with her older sister. So it was just "Little Guy" and me. We rented a basement suite in North Vancouver, near Capilano Road, so it was only a mile or so to work.

The New Farrell 32

I was facing a hell of a big challenge getting the plug and all the moulds built and a boat built and ready for fishing season, but I was game, even though this meant starting from scratch again in 1982 at the age of forty-eight. There was no café near the shop, which in one way was a good thing (no breaks). I would get up at five in the morning, make a big pot of porridge, have a bowl and put the rest in plastic containers and take them to work for lunch and supper. I'd work from six in the morning till ten or eleven at night. I know it wasn't fair to my son—the fact that I was working all those hours and not being home for him—but he was ten years old and a pretty capable guy. In the winter, he'd head up Grouse Mountain every chance he had to go skiing. One winter he went up about fifty times. He also became quite streetwise at an early age. There wasn't much I could do as I had taken on this obligation.

My former employee at Nanoose, Roy Brown, who now owned Independent Shipwrights in Coombs, had acquired some of my old moulds for the thirty-two. I'm not sure how he got them, but he was good friends with Don Piccolo, who had taken over my Nanoose shop, so I cheated a bit and made arrangements to borrow the cabin, cabin top and back deck moulds from him. I rented a five-ton truck and went over to Coombs and got them all on one load, with Roy being kind enough to load them with his machine. I made a lot of changes and smoothed and revamped the parts I took out of them, then I took new moulds off the parts.

When I made the hull plug, I used all different materials, whichever suited the shape the best: quarter-inch plywood around the transom, Melamine on the sides and the straight runs on the aft part, narrow tongue-and-groove on the bottom at the bow where it was convex, and then regular cedar planking on the flare at the bow.

The new Farrell 32 (left), next to an old Farrell 32. Quite a difference.

Now, most guys at this stage would put a layer of fibreglass over the whole plug and spend a week or two filling and sanding and painting, but I just smoothed the wood down, and there's a product I love called Duratec. It's a high-build polyester primer that goes on really thick and is very easy to sand. I sprayed the plug with that and in a day or so had it all sanded down. Another quality of Duratec is that it will polish to a mirror shine, so I shone her up, waxed her and took a mould off her. I got help for a week or so laying up the fibreglass and then it took another couple of weeks to strengthen it. I put plywood ribs on the outside of the mould and built two big half-circle tracks for it to roll from side to side on wheels on the cradle so you could simply walk in and do the layup. The hull mould turned out far more fair and with crisper lines than any mould I had made so far.

It's hard to explain just how labour-intensive and strenuous all the hand sanding and preparation of the parts was in order to take the moulds off. During the long hours, working alone and sometimes working late at night when I would be driving myself, I would almost feel like crying, but I would keep pushing myself. I should have hired someone to help but I knew if I kept going the way I was going, I would have just enough money to pull it off.

I pulled the hull mould off the plug and dragged the plug outside, turned the mould over and got it into the cart I had built ahead of time with wheels on the top and bottom and began sanding it, cut-polishing it and then waxing it. Then it was ready to lay up the first hull, so I hired a couple of guys for the fibreglassing of the hull.

The new plug for the Farrell 32 is just about finished, built at my North Vancouver shop in 1982. It is a shame to make such a thing of beauty and then chop it up and throw it away after the mould is taken off it.

After that was done, came the finishing of the boat. While I was installing the engine, shaft, rudder, shoe, fuel tanks and a lot of other stuff, I hired a fellow to do the finishing in the cabin. His name was Hubert "Joe" Van Bergen, and he was working at Alberni Shipyards in 1950 when I was an apprentice there. I hadn't seen him since then. I was also installing the command bridge, visor and trim on the hull. When it came to the wiring and hydraulics, my buddy Ralph Rolston, from Seair Marine, dropped what he was doing and came to my rescue and he did all that for me. Wayne Murdock, a top-notch machinist and welder who used to work at Wagner Engineering, did all the metal work: stainless steel rudder and shoe, aluminum mast, poles and railings. Queensboro Marine made the drum, rollers and anchor winch for me. We put a little six-cylinder Volvo diesel in her. Anyway, I got her finished pretty well on schedule— it was a week into fishing season, but there were no fish yet, so it was okay. The boat was named *Kirstin F* and she did great on the sea trials. She also floated just right. I hadn't kept any line drawings for the first thirty-two I'd been building in Richmond, so I had to pretty well design this one from scratch again and you always worry a little bit about it, so I was a happy man. When everything was finished and the bills were all paid, I broke even (I was broke, but even) and I had the moulds. Len gave me a $500 bonus so I had a bit of money to take a little break. When Len headed north fishing, I got a ride with him to False Bay on Lasqueti Island and visited my dad on his

Me waxing and polishing the mould for the new Farrell 32.

boat *China Cloud*. Len stayed the night and headed out the next morning. I stayed with Dad and Sharie for a few days. I sure needed a rest. I had lost a lot of weight and was dragging my butt.

After Len's boat got out on the fishing grounds, the orders started coming in. The first two were kit boats (with the engines, shaft, rudder, fuel tanks, windows, visor and trim on the hull) for the Nomura brothers, Richard and John, who were Steveston fishermen. The boats were named *Count the Green* and *Prime Time III*. Their brother Hiro, who was a good boat finisher, helped finish them.

The next boat was for Pender Harbour fisherman Allen Scoular, Bill Scoular's son. It was the only boat I built with the top of the window sloping forward. Allen drew a sketch of the cabin he wanted and I made the changes to a cabin out of my mould. Allen was a good guy to have around and I let him rough in the interior of his cabin in my shop. I was always preaching to guys that if you want to go fast and save fuel, you have to keep them light, but Allen knew this and he did a good job of it. I remember when the boat was finished and he brought it to Vancouver. I was having a look at it and he said, "You see that ceiling up there, it only weighs twenty-six pounds, including screws." When Allen's boat got up to twenty-three knots or so (full speed), it would list to one side or another. I tried to remedy it, but no luck. The boat wasn't designed to do more than twenty knots with that keel I had on her. Allen wasn't too concerned about it anyway. As far as I know, none of my other boats did that.

Allen Scoular's Miss Pender. *This was the only boat I built with forward sloping windows.*

I could go on about each boat I built, but I won't. I was booked solid each year for the next three. I was just building kit boats; they went elsewhere for finishing, so I could do about one boat a month. I usually had a couple of guys working with me. I was getting the hulls laid up at Steveston Fibreglass (where the Vancouver 27s had been laid up) and we were laying up the deck/cabin and all the other parts, and of course doing the assembly. There was just enough room in my shop on Bewicke Avenue to assemble a kit boat and be laying the cabin/deck for the next one. I built a Quonset addition on the back of my shop to lay up the command bridges, back caps and other moulded pieces.

I went ahead and built a boat for a guy up north with only the down payment and a promise that the money was coming through right away, but the money didn't come through, so the next guy in line was to get it. His name was Don Frinski and he was a fisherman from Surrey. I had put a 3208 Cat diesel in it, but Don wanted a different model Cat. He had a shipwright friend who was helping him with the finishing, so they changed engines and the "expert" told Don the engine beds weren't big and strong enough. He was from the old school and figured they had to be heavy angle iron the full length of the engine, so they changed them. Don told me later that they took the bolts out and had a hell of a time getting the ones I put in loose from the fibreglass stringers. They had to use wedges and sledgehammers and it took them a few hours. I used to get steel angle brackets made up about a foot long with gussets in for each mount. I would rough up the steel and bear shit (resin mixed with asbestos to thicken it up) and bolt them into the hollow fibreglass stringers. Of the three hundred or so boats I built, I never had any trouble.

With the last dozen or so thirty-two-footers I built, I switched to aluminum mounts and put in some pretty big engines (a V8-71 in one). Some of my boats hit sheer rock bluffs and others hit the beach and went on up into the woods and the mounts stood up, so enough said.

The way I got rigidity in the decks was to take a sheet of plywood and rough it up really good with a twenty-four grit sanding disk on the grinder (to insure a good bond), then cut the sheet into three-and-a-half-inch blocks and bond them down with a well-saturated one-and-a-half-ounce fibreglass mat in the mould. After it hardened, I'd sand it down and put one-and-a-half-ounce

My thirty-two-footer, the second True North, *doing 24 knots.*

mat over it. A fellow who owned a boat building shop in Steveston and who did some fine fibreglass layups, came to my shop one day while I was doing this and said I was doing it wrong and that I should be putting a mat-roving-mat over the blocks, but three hundred boats and many years later, the decks are standing up just fine, so again, enough said.

5

Older and Wiser

In 1986, Vancouver was preparing to host the world's fair, Expo 86. I got busy, got a hunk of wood and started whittling a two-foot model of my thirty-seven, and after I had whittled the cabin, bridge and all the other parts, I made a full set of moulds for them. I built a few of these little buggers and completed one with remote controls and all the rigging as a combination troller/gillnetter. The poles lowered for trolling and the cabin top and back deck lifted off to get at the servos and motor. A good friend of mine, Ron Burchett, is a super model maker and he helped with the remote part of things. He was having a radio-controlled boat display in a big pond at Expo 86 and he took my model to show with his other boats. I used to go over and play with it once in a while.

The two-foot radio-controlled model I built for Expo 86.

Drawing up Plans

Howard Gray, a Prince Rupert fisherman, had bought a thirty-seven from me while I was still in Richmond and he had it finished at Ralph Rolston's Seair Marine. He had it for a few years and then it burned up on him and he wanted another thirty-seven, but no one was building them anymore. He got in touch with me and said he could get one built out of aluminum by Shore Boatbuilders (a well-known aluminum seine boat builder in Richmond) if I could supply the blueprints. However, I designed my boats using sketches and I didn't keep them, 'cause once you build a mould, you don't figure you'll need it again. Anyway, Shore commissioned me to draw up a new set of plans for them. They asked me how much I'd charge and I said five hundred bucks. I've never had any education in boat design, but I figured out all the buttock lines and waterlines by looking at other blueprints and included them so the plans looked like a real professional did them. When it comes to education, I'm just a grade six dropout, but I can figure things out. There wasn't much money in it at five hundred. The only other plans I drew up for other people were the plans for Sonny Reid's thirty-eight-foot gillnetter, *Instigator*, built by Denny Harling at Garden Bay Boat Works in 1967. I drew up a lot of other boat plans, but they were all for boats I built.

Extra Sensory Perception

I've had a lot of ESP experiences throughout my life. My dad and me seemed to have a connection. One time while I was building *Klyuhk* for Henry Whittaker at Irvines Landing, I was thinking about Dad and thinking that I hadn't seen him or heard from him for about six months or so. I stopped work and walked out to the point and there he was, sailing down the strait.

My dad was a good artist and sometimes when I would be visiting him, and maybe someone else would be there too, we'd all grab a brush and copy Dad as he painted a scene. Mine turned out pretty good and I began to think I would like to take up painting someday when I wasn't so busy building boats.

Anyway, I was driving along one day in North Vancouver and I had a vision of a bright yellow sky, the sea and trees and I thought to myself I'd like to paint that. I went to visit Dad a week or so later and here's the painting of the yellow sky and dark trees. I said, "You know what, Dad? I had a vision of that about a week ago. The only difference was that my trees were coming out on the other side of the painting." He said that was strange because he did another painting of the same yellow sky and trees a week ago—and the trees were coming from the other side of it.

I was working in my shop on Bewicke Avenue and hadn't seen or heard from Dad for quite a while, so I thought to myself, I think I'll try mental telepathy. I started saying over and over, "phone me, Dad," while looking in the sky towards where he was. Sure enough in about half an hour, the phone rang and it was Dad. Now, I don't know if it was the mental telepathy thing or maybe I just had a premonition that he was going to phone.

When I lived at Irvines Landing and was building *Klyuck,* I loaned my sixteen-foot speedboat to one of the hippie couples to go to Lloyds Store in Garden Bay. I watched as they came back in and were making a landing. They had landed perfectly and everything looked fine but for some reason I had a premonition that something was going to go wrong. I went running out the back of my shop and down to the float just as the accident happened. Somehow the guy had jammed the throttle full ahead and my boat had smashed up onto the stern of the boat ahead. The guy who owned the other boat was there and made a big to-do about it, but there wasn't a lot of damage.

The uncle of a girlfriend of mine was having an operation in Nanaimo. It wasn't that serious an operation, but I sensed that he didn't make it and after the operation she came over from Nanaimo to spend the weekend with me.

When she showed up at my shop on Bewicke Avenue, the first thing I said to her was, "I know."

Another time the same girl and me were driving up to Zeballos on the west coast of Vancouver Island. I had a friend that I hadn't seen for a few years and he had a house south of Parksville. I decided to stop by. However, a few miles before we got to his house, I had a premonition the house was gone. I started wondering what happened to it, whether it had burned or was moved or if it had been torn down. Sure enough, when we drove past, the house was gone.

My buddy Pete Hansen was a logger and for quite a few years he worked up north at various camps, usually for different lengths of time. For years, every time I'd pick up the phone to call him, he'd say, "I just walked in the door to my apartment. How the hell did you know?"

These are just a few of the dozens and dozens of experiences I've had.

Birthday Surprise

After I got the new moulds for the thirty-two done, a coffee shop called the High Boat Café opened up at Mosquito Creek Marina. It had an entrance on Bewicke Avenue, by my shop, and one in the marina. It was first opened by a fellow named Dave Lloyd and then bought by Cathy Chambers. Cathy was a lot of fun and did a great job of running the place. She had different things for lunch on certain days (it was all good food and her fish chowder was excellent) and was open seven days a week. She had a fantastic memory. As the customers came to the counter to order, she would ask their names and the next time they came in she would call them by name. There was a long table in the middle where all the locals and other friends like Al Brown, Jim Caplette, Jack Munro, Jim Sinclair and all the boat builders and fishermen sat, and of course me and my crew. It was a real boater's café. Cathy and the boys got together and decided to give me a treat for my birthday. I was sitting at the café a day before my birthday, so I didn't suspect anything (they'd gotten the date wrong) and this beautiful redhead came in and stood across the table from me. She said, "Hi, Barrie, don't you remember me? We had such a good time in Nanaimo." I said, "No." The place was packed and I couldn't figure out why. The redhead had a ghetto blaster with her and she set it on the table and started dancing and her clothes started coming off. I was so embarrassed. I said, "I just want to eat my lunch." Anyway, after all her clothes were off, except for panties and bra, she came over and sat on my knee. If she'd only known that I'd been grinding fibreglass all morning, she wouldn't have. I bet she had an itchy bum.

Politics

At this time, Prime Minister Brian Mulroney was pushing through the so-called "Free Trade" deal with the States. There was an organic grain farmer from Saskatoon named David Orchard who was a crusader in the fight against it. When he came to Vancouver for a rally, I went to it. I was impressed with him so I joined his group Citizens Concerned About Free Trade (CAFT). I went to all the meetings, joined in a lot of protests and donated quite a bit of money towards it. One time Mulroney came to Vancouver on his big tour bus and we met it. I got to within about fifteen feet of him and had my hands cupped to my face shouting, "Traitor! Traitor!" I was deeply involved with the group for some time. Well, we got the free trade in 1994 and I don't believe it has worked out too well for Canada.

Before it became official, David was gaining momentum in the anti-free-trade movement right across Canada. He would have up to twelve hundred people at his meetings. Perhaps it was because Mulroney was seeing the writing on the wall that he called a snap election. David spoke the common man's language with a lot of common sense. People could tell he was an honest man who wouldn't compromise his principles. And he had all the facts about the negative side of the free trade deal. He was so dedicated that he sold his herd of cattle (which he was raising along with his organic grain) and used the money to fight the deal.

The press were told not to give him any coverage, so David figured the only way to get the word out about what was happening in Canadian politics was to become the leader of a political party, so he joined the leadership race for the Progressive Conservative Party. There were five guys running and David was in second place (pretty good for a grain farmer who had never been in politics before). On voting day, David came in second on the first round of voting. Then two of the candidates joined forces, so that put David in third place, but it also made him the king-maker. If he put his support behind Peter McKay on the second ballot, Peter would win. But before he did, he drew up an agreement for Peter to sign—with certain stipulations, one of them being that the PCs would not join up with the Alliance Party. He had the document properly witnessed and made legal, but soon after, McKay started negotiating with the Alliance Party's Stephen Harper to join up. He literally destroyed the PC party. Peter stabbed David in the back despite the legal document he had signed.

Anyway, before that there was a big PC convention happening in Edmonton and David asked me to be a delegate for him. I got to hob-nob with some pretty important people like John Crosbie, Joe Clark and others. Before I went back there, I was having coffee with Jack Munro, the IWA union leader, and he said that when Joe Clark was out here, they hit it off good and he asked me to say hello for him if I saw Joe, which I did.

In my eyes, David Orchard is an unsung hero.

True North

I decided to build myself a thirty-two-footer and I slipped it in between other production. I named her *True North*, after the newspaper put out by the Citizens Concerned About Free Trade. At the time I was putting a lot of Cummins engines in the boats I built, so when it came to my engine, Brian Thomas, a friend who I'd gone to school with in Pender Harbour, and who was now a partner in the company that distributed Cummins diesels where'd I'd been buying my engines, got me my engine at an unbelievably low price and I put all the best electronics on her. I got my buddy Ralph Rolston to do the wiring and hydraulics. Everything was installed, even the upholstery, but I just roughed in the interior.

Then came my big launching day. Gary Nahanee, then manager of Mosquito Creek Marina, brought the travel lift out of the marina and onto Bewicke Avenue, and down the road to my shop. He picked up *True North* and took it back to the marina for launching. He really bent the rules for me. Good old Gary.

There were a lot of people at the launching and my stepdaughter Mitzi christened her and down into the water she went. Brian Thomas, the fellow who'd sold me the engine, was there to do the start-up, as was Ralph, who'd done the hydraulics and wiring and the electric

My stepdaughter, Mitzi, christening the True North *at Mosquito Creek Marina.*

engine controls. Something seemed to be wrong, so the guys disconnected the throttle control at the gear lever. For some reason, when they started it, the diesel ran away and went to full rpms. Instead of turning the key off, one of them grabbed the throttle lever and pulled it back. Well, the throttle wasn't connected, just hanging there, and it happened to hit the gear lever and slam the boat into gear wide open. The boat was still tied facing the travel lift dock. Now, being a light boat, she jumped half out of the water, broke the tie-up line, and went at great speed into the dock.

There was quite a few people on board and it flattened everybody. I was standing at the back of the cabin and I remember being airborne and landing in the cockpit with my head against the stern. Dean Crosby (who was working for me and was the son of Fred Crosby, the builder from Pender Harbour) landed in the cockpit with his back against the rail and when we hit the dock, it threw him the full length of the deck and he hit his face on the cabin back. It was just lucky that the tide was where it was and that there was a timber sticking out at the right height so that when the boat smashed into it, it punched a hole in the bulwarks and stopped the boat. Otherwise she would have kept going and probably wiped the cabin off and maybe killed someone. Of course Ralph and Brian were on the floor in the cabin, but one of them managed to get up and turn the key off. My grandson Justin was standing on the float, hanging onto the rail of the boat when it took off and he got dragged between the boat and float and was underwater somewhere for quite a while. Finally my son, Allen, spotted him on the bottom under the ramp of the float and dove in and got him. We got him up to the hospital and he was okay, except for his leg being munched up a bit. He still has the scars.

Here was my new boat with the bulwarks all smashed in. I guess I should have been upset and angry, but I just said, "Shit happens, guys." I guess I was just thankful that no one was badly hurt. I got a young fellow who had experience installing electric controls down to the boat the same afternoon and he got the problem solved in no time and away we went on the sea trials. She did twenty-four knots.

I just threw a rough fibreglass patch over the hole in the bulwarks and used her that way. I used to get over to visit my dad on his boat quite often, either at Lasqueti Island or in Nanaimo Harbour. I'd take people over to the Keg restaurant at False Creek. I quite enjoyed the *True North*.

Because I was busy at the time, I didn't have time to repair her, but the next spring things slowed down a bit and I put her behind my shop and did the repairs. The insurance paid and I completely finished the interior and went all out on her. I was pretty proud of her when I got through.

I had rented a large lower suite in Pemberton Heights (North Vancouver) and had a couple of the kids living with me. They were in their teens and kind of wild, so I moved onto the boat and left the suite to them. I liked living aboard at Mosquito Creek. Gary, the manager, had put cablevision and telephone down to the docks.

Mosquito Creek used to be a lot different during the seventeen years I was there. It used to be bigger and a lot more casual. There were a few guys living on their boats up on the hard, some living under tarp lean-tos while they worked on their boats. They used to have a big bonfire, roasting wieners, drinking beer, playing guitar and singing. I would join them some-

Fuelling up True North.

times (that was after the first year when I was too busy building the mould and finishing the first boat). But no beer drinking for me, I was on the wagon then and stayed on it for twenty-five years.

The marina staff would line up the old derelict boats in a row behind my shop. They called it death row. They had a big pit where they would push them in and burn them. They'd get a couple pushed in and ready for burning before lunch and then come back after lunch and torch them. They wouldn't take anything off them so there was a lot of good stuff aboard and I'd go out there during lunch hour and get a lot of stuff off them: toilets, steering wheels, cleats, doors and all kinds of goodies. I would take the stuff to Popeye's Sailors Exchange next door to me and they would sell it for me.

A New Wife

Bill Harrison, who had a store at the marina that opened both onto Bewicke Avenue and the Marina, sold paint and fibreglass materials—and had a Chinese girl-friend. One day I said, "You know, Bill, I wouldn't mind meeting a Chinese girl," so they invited me up to their apartment for supper. Bill's girlfriend and a girl named Li had cooked up a fancy twelve-or-so course Chinese meal. After supper we went out for a cruise in the harbour on *True North* and Li and me hit it off, although she had only been here a few months from Shanghai, China, and couldn't speak much English. We started phoning and dating. The day before Christmas, she was standing on the dock visiting me while I was getting ready to go over and spend Christmas with my dad. I asked her what she was going to do for Christmas and she said, "I will follow you." It touched me (it reminded me of that nice song "I

It may be snowing outside, but it's cozy inside. This was taken when Li and I were living aboard.

My wife, Li, Sharie Farrell and me aboard Allen and Sharie's junk China Cloud *in the early 1990s.*

Will Follow You") so I said, "Jump aboard." And away we went to dad and Sharie's and spent a beautiful Christmas with them in their floathouse in False Bay on Lasqueti, where Dad was building the twenty-seven-foot sailboat *August Moon.* After Christmas, Li moved onto the boat with me and got a job at a plastic moulding place on the east side of the Second Narrows Bridge.

We lived on *True North* for a few years, and then a guy offered me a price that I couldn't refuse, so I sold her. Then I bought an aluminum Cruise-A-Home—kind of a fast, fifteen-knot houseboat—with a new 454 Olds engine in her. We made one trip to Nanaimo in it. It cost $250 for gas, and that was back when gas was a lot cheaper. When we got back to Mosquito Creek, I took a look at the engine and said, "I guess you'll stay new as long as I've got you, you bloody guzzler."

The Last Thirty-two

The last thirty-two I built was for a fellow named Cliff Jackman. Cliff was a nice fellow who had a vegetable farm on Turner Road, north of Nanaimo. He was an ex-land surveyor and commercial troller. The thing about Cliff was that it took him a long time to make up his mind. He came into my shop to order a thirty-two-foot troller, but after an hour or so of questions, he said he'd better go home and think this over. He came back a week or so later and we went through the same routine. Then he phoned me from his home and said, "If you're going to be on the Island, drop in. I'm ready to sign." So I stopped at his place and spent a bunch more time going over it all again and again. He said to leave the contract with him and he'd go over things. My contracts were two pages long, with only the bare necessities. I was used to fishermen coming into the shop and saying, "I want to order a boat. Where do I sign?" I was going to the Island again so I phoned Cliff and he said, "Yes, stop in. I think I'm ready to sign." Well, he'd written a small book with fifty-seven paragraphs of stipulations, which we had to go over and both initial each paragraph. Finally he signed.

Cliff wanted me to look after the finishing of the boat, so I built the kit and subcontracted the finishing to Brian Wahl (one of Ernest Wahl's sons) on River Road in Richmond. Things went good on the boat for a while, then about halfway through, it kind of came to a standstill. Brian had financial problems and he had other jobs on the go and every time I'd go over to check on progress, nothing was done. The last time I went over, here was a guy dismantling the electronics and taking them away. I said, "Hey, hold on! What the hell is going on?" The guy said, "Well, he never paid me," so I said, "Well, don't worry. I'll pay you. Let's not go backward anymore." I'd given Brian a big cash advance to cover all that stuff and more. So I went to lunch with Brian and said, "I guess I better take the boat back to my shop, eh Brian?" And he said, "Yeah, I guess you better, Barrie." I had overpaid Brian, so there wasn't much money left to finish her and Cliff was a very meticulous man. He said in his contract that everything must be extra accessible, as he was getting a bit crotchety. It took me about two months to finish her. I could have built a couple of kit boats in that time, but she turned out nice. He wanted her for Gulf (Strait of Georgia) trolling but right after she was finished, Fisheries closed the Gulf for trolling permanently, so Cliff sold her. She is called *Gulf Wanderer* and is tied up at the government dock at Ganges on Salt Spring Island. She is owned by John and Verna Elliott and they look after her well. That last time I saw her, she looked brand new.

Building the Thirty-four

I had been busy all along building thirty-twos, but things slowed down a bit so I decided to build a set of moulds for a thirty-four by twelve-foot model with a pleasure boat cabin that could be blocked off in the mould and used as a commercial fishboat as well. I brought a thirty-two hull into the shop and cut it up to use for the plug. I cut the stern off and cut it down the middle. Then I cut the chine the full length of the boat and cut

Here, I'm in the process of lengthening the Farrell 32 mould (to thirty-four feet) and widening it (to twelve feet, two inches) for use as a pleasure boat. This was the last mould I made—and the hardest.

it along the bulwarks and hung them by wires from the rafters. There was an awful lot of grinding to bevel every joint. I figured out after a while that it was a hard way to make a plug, all that grinding. The only advantage was that the plug could be a boat when I was through, but it still wasn't worth it. I did the cabin, bridge and cabin top the same way, and built the aft part of the cabin from scratch to make it a pleasure boat. It's a lot of work making a set of moulds.

A friend of mine, Mike West from Pender Harbour, came into the shop while I was building the mould. I had the hull mould built and was building the cabin on the hull plug to take the mould off. It was at the stage where it didn't look so great, but Mike had a friend, Joe Edger, with him. Joe was looking for a pleasure boat and they'd been looking at Cliff's thirty-two-footer out in the marina. Joe looked over what I was doing and the drawings of the finished product and said, "I'll take one. I'll be around tomorrow with some money for you." That made me happy because it enabled me to finish the moulds. Joe was an excellent customer. We put a 400-hp C-series Cummins diesel in her. Joe named her *Casa Jose* and she did twenty-seven knots on the sea trials. I had roughed in the interior and was working on her behind my shop. I had all the stainless steel railings and radar arch made up by Blue Water Rigging ($16,000). When I built the sink counter, I kind of screwed up and got it too low, so I just told people the customer's wife was a midget.

A guy by the name of Dave Letson ordered a thirty-four before I got Joe's boat out of the shop. I had shipped the hull mould over to Steveston Fibreglass and they laid up a dark blue hull for me while I laid up a grey and white cabin and deck. Dave lived in Sidney on Vancouver Island and was the wharfinger at Hot Springs Cove north of Tofino and used the boat for the job. He did a nice job of the layout and the finishing of *Dieflyn*, which means "little devil" in Welsh. He told me a while ago that since he retired he's cruised far into Alaska four times. He was telling me about a bunch of his boating buddies and how they formed a club they call "The Princess Louisa Bible Society." In the middle of winter ten or so boats would head up from Sidney on Vancouver Island to Princess Louisa Inlet, near the top of Jervis Inlet, for a week or so on a booze cruise. One winter they were heading home and hit a bad southeaster, and they all holed up in Secret Cove on the Sunshine Coast—except Dave. Out of all the other boats, he was the only one who continued across to Nanaimo. Dave had the boat for seventeen years, but age finally caught up with him and maintaining the boat became too much, so he recently sold her to a couple from Alaska. While he had her, he put on 35,208 nautical miles.

My shop on Bewicke Avenue was just wide enough to build the thirty-twos, cabin and hull, side by side, but now with the new thirty-four being nineteen inches wider, I couldn't do it anymore. I decided to find a shop somewhere on Vancouver Island, so I phoned Roy Brown at Independent Shipwrights and asked him to keep an eye open for a shop for me.

I got another order for a thirty-four with a short cabin sport fisher with a low back deck and a box over the engine outside, adjoining the cabin. The customer also wanted a deck alongside the box at the sheerline level for his kid to sleep in, accessible from inside the cabin. It was for Darrell Spring, who had a place in Pender

The Dieflyn *with engine installed and ready for Dave Letson to finish her. Dave is standing at the bow.*

Harbour and owned a trucking company in Coquitlam called Wheeler Transport.

I did a complete kit boat for him and he took it to his work yard and had Richmond boat builder Hiro Namura finish it. Hiro did a nice job on her, but it ended up a little heavy in the cabin area and floated a little high in the stern. But she performed well and they did a nice write-up on her in *Pacific Yachting* magazine. The young fellow loved his "cubbyhole." This was the last boat I built in North Vancouver.

Coombs

Roy Brown phoned me and said he was building a big new high building at his place in Coombs with four bays in it and wondered if I'd be interested in renting a couple of them. I agreed. I was lucky because Darrell Spring helped me with his trucking company. He brought a forty-foot container and parked it behind my shop so I could load everything from the shop into it.

I'd been to the dentist and had some teeth pulled and a plate made up. While I was working, I took them out and put them in my shirt pocket. In the evening, I noticed they were gone. So, for the next couple of days, I kept an eye out for them, as they'd cost me almost a thousand bucks, but I couldn't find them.

One evening, I was working by myself and I was having a pee behind the shop where we'd been loading stuff into the container. We'd been using a little forklift and dug up the ground pretty good, so it was quite deep dust. While I was peeing, all of a sudden something white and shiny showed up. Ah, ha, my teeth. Discovered by my own Geiger counter.

When we were all loaded up, Darrell came with a semi and took the container to the new shop on Vancouver Island and left it there for a week or so while we unloaded. He did all this out of the kindness of his heart.

Roy asked me if the shop was okay and I said I would like a mezzanine floor in the back part of it. He got his crew, some timbers and a forklift and threw up a mezzanine with a set of stairs in record time. I was amazed how quick they got it up. Then I went ahead and built an office, lunchroom and storage room under it.

To get started, I had a couple of orders for fishboats out of the new mould, but then Howard Vestad (son of Ole Vestad), who was first in line, came over in person to give me the bad news that there had been changes in the fishing licence regulations and he would have to cancel his order. Then another fisherman, Ben Jenkins, phoned and cancelled his order. It seemed that in the mid-1990s, there was a glut of used fibreglass boats on the market and changes in licensing meant speed was no longer the most important factor in the commercial salmon fishing industry.

I had Joe Edger's boat, *Casa Jose*, in the shop for finishing and I went ahead and built a hull out of the mould (which sat outside the shop for a long time). So, the move to the Island didn't turn out that good. My intention, when I rented from Roy, was to build new boats, but it didn't work out that way. I got *Casa Jose*

The Casa Jose, *a thirty-four-foot pleasure boat version with the full-length cabin. This was built from the plug for the thirty-four mould. Top speed was about twenty-seven knots.*

completed and other work came in, but it was no hell. I rented a house in Parksville, and Allen and his buddy (who were working for me), my stepdaughter and her boyfriend and her girlfriend were all living there, so for peace and quiet, I moved to my office and lived there for a long time. I did a lot of repair work, but Roy was well established with the fishermen around there and got most of the work.

Allen and me got some interesting work in, though. One job we landed through French Creek Boat Sales (now Pacific Boat Brokers) was for Universal Studios in Japan. We took four old boats from different trades and stripped them of the engines, fuel tanks and all the toxic stuff. One boat was a wooden tug, *Strady IX*, another was an old gillnetter, the third was a troller and the fourth was a steel tug. All the rot had to be repaired and the boats had to be painted up in pretty colours specified by Universal Studios. The wooden hull on the troller had to be fibreglassed. The boats were going to go in a pond in a theme park in Tokyo.

I got an order for a thirty-four-foot pleasure boat from a nice fellow named Bill Wheeler. I took a contract for a finished boat. During the finishing, Bill would bring his girlfriend and she would suggest changes. Finally I said, "Bill, I'm going to have to start charging you for the changes." The changes amounted to $17,000. The boat is named *Kingfisher* and I think he recently sold it and bought a sailboat. There was a lot of sophisticated electronics on the boat, which I'm not into, so I got an electrician who I was led to believe was good. But when the boat got to Campbell River, there were a few bugs in the installations and the company that was hired to fix the problems spread the word that the whole boat was flawed (human nature, I guess). It's too bad Bill didn't have some input into the wiring end of things, as he is an electronics whiz and a very capable builder. Anyway, Bill has had the boat for almost twenty years now and has been really happy with it.

A funny thing happened while I was building Bill's boat. I also had a thirty-six-foot gillnetter belonging to Jack Jenson in my shop. I was putting on a new bow section where it had been smashed in. Jack was preparing the whole boat for spray painting. When I first gave Jack a price on painting the whole boat, he thought it was too much but after prepping the boat himself, he said, "Holy cow! Now I see why it costs so much—all the filling, sanding, getting into every nook and cranny by hand, dismantling stuff to get at places and all the masking. Wow!"

Anyway, back to the funny thing. I had hired a top-notch finisher from Qualicum who usually did finishing on high-end houses and was from the upper crust of society. Now, Jack was more of a rugged fisherman type with socialist ideas and he would get ranting in the lunchroom at lunchtime, waving his arms about and such. Well, this elite finishing guy came to me and said, "I think I'm going to have to quit because I'm afraid of Jack."

Another boat I had in my shop at the time was Norm Jones' gillnetter *Midnight Lady*. Norm was having me extend his cabin to make it into a pleasure boat and also put one of my command bridges on her. Norm is kind of a crusty character and a good friend. He is a good guitar player and singer and had his own band at one time. He now has a forty-foot tugboat, named *Westcoaster,* and a 176-foot barge to go with her.

The next and last order was for a thirty-four-foot gillnetter for Randy Dudoward. He was also a good gentleman to deal with. (I've actually been lucky through the years with all the good customers I've had.) After Randy's boat, things went slack. I figured if the company couldn't even get through a slack period after all the long hours and hard work I'd put in, I might as well pack it in, but when I mentioned it to my son, he said, "What am I going to do?" I gave him the company, but things didn't turn out so good for him either, and that was the end of Farrell Boats.

I then sold the moulds to Eric Benfield in Coombs and went to work for him. He had a fibreglass business building sundecks and repairing fibreglass boats. I worked for him for five years until his business ran down too. The moulds were eventually crushed and scrapped.

Piecework in Vancouver

All the time I'd been running the business in Coombs, my common-law wife, Li, continued working in North Vancouver and living at my dear Aunt Kay's in West Vancouver. Kay was my dad's sister. I went back over to West Vancouver and took it easy for a week or so. Then I decided it was time to get back to work, so I spread the word at the High Boat Café at the Mosquito Creek Marina and within twenty minutes, I had landed a job.

It was with George McNealy who had struck it rich in the stock market and was restoring a forty-two-foot wooden Monk-designed yacht built in 1953. I joined a couple of the top-notch marine finishers including Don McLeod, who was the best I'd ever worked with, and was told "spare no expense." We used all the most exotic woods such as ebony, jarrah, padouk, Honduras mahogany, yellow cedar, blue gumwood and others. I was told, "Just use your imagination and do your thing." It was a fun job and we made a beautiful job of her. George built a boathouse for his boat with a suite above.

Once that job was finished I rebuilt a thirty-two-foot sailboat designed by Ben Seaborn, the guy who designed the very popular twenty-six-foot Thunderbird sailboat. His boats were very successful but he ended up committing suicide.

After that, I took the job of lengthening a thirty-eight-foot Zeta catamaran powerboat to forty-seven feet. The hull was cored and the outer fibreglass was thinner than the inner, so it was difficult to join. The fellow who owns it now told me they go north in her in the summers and have been through some heavy-duty storms and she's standing up good—and does thirty-eight knots!

While I was working on that job, my dad got pneumonia and died just a few months short of his ninetieth birthday. Up until then he was still in great shape. He was living on his forty-foot Chinese junk, *China Cloud*, which he'd built. He was anchored tucked in Daisy's Lagoon, off False Bay on Lasqueti Island. During low tides at night in the winter, he'd be high and dry and say, "Let 'er blow!" He was a gentle man who treaded lightly on this earth. He had a magnetic personality and had a lot of followers. There was no engine in *China Cloud* (that's the way he built her), but he would still go sailing every chance he got. He'd haul anchor and hoist the sails by hand. When there was no wind, he'd scull her by hand with a big twenty-foot-long oar. He could still beat the average guy in a foot race at almost ninety years old. When I was working at Mosquito Creek, after the Coombs experience, I would take every second Thursday off and catch the two ferries over to visit him. I would get a barbecued chicken and a bunch of growlies to take to him. I loved my old dad immensely. When he'd give you a hug goodbye, it felt like a bear had got hold of you. My Aunt Lois died a week before he died. They both left me some money, so Li and I decided to buy a sailboat and bugger off.

Cruising

We bought a forty-foot ketch, *Marana*. She wasn't in bad shape, but we decided to renew everything in her except the engine. My good buddy Ralph took two weeks off and rewired the whole boat for us (no charge, much appreciated!). Good old Ralph.

I took Li's relations out on *Marana* for a day cruise and we went up into False Creek. I was cruising along at a fast idle. I'd been up to the head of the creek dozens of times with *True North* and I wasn't thinking about my tall mast and the low clearance under the Cambie Street Bridge (again, pretty stupid). Anyway, *bam*! I hit the bridge with the mast and the bow came way up in the air and then we kind of spun around. The only thing that happened was the steering cable came off inside the helm console and that's a place that is hard to get to. I got the boat anchored and got busy fixing the steering. I was lucky no one got hurt

My dad, Allen Farrell, at the age of eighty-five.

Allen Farrell's last boat, the forty-foot junk, China Cloud, *one of some forty vessels he built on the beach with only hand tools.*

and not much damage. I felt so stupid and I never told anyone about it until now.

Another time I took Li's relations and friends out on *Marana* for a sail out of Comox on Vancouver Island. We were sailing back into the harbour and the roller furling for the genoa got tangled up, so I rushed to the bow to fix it, but she was tangled up pretty good. I'd put one guy on the wheel, and one watching the sounder so I was telling the guy on the wheel when to turn and the other guy was shouting soundings to me—"twenty feet, fifteen feet, ten feet,"—and next thing I know, we're stuck on a sandbar. The tide was dropping and it was blowing pretty good. At first I kind of panicked and called the Coast Guard (big mistake). Pretty soon there's this big old Buffalo search and rescue plane circling around and then the local Coast Guard auxiliary boat came out from the harbour. I told them I was going to be okay and was just going to row an anchor out and wait for the tide to come back in. But they said no, and put a line on me and went out into deeper water and waited for the tide. I had eleven people aboard and I only had a few life jackets, so I had Li's nephew, Too Too, ferrying people in to the dock in the little dinghy. He could only take a couple at a time, just in case the Coast Guard checked me out. After we got free, the Coast Guard came alongside and said a lot of people get stuck on that bar. I asked them if I owed them anything and they said no, that they were local volunteers, but they would accept donations. So I thanked them very much and stopped by their office the next morning to give them a couple hundred dollars.

After a while, it was finally time to bugger off and head north to go cruising. As we passed under the Lions Gate Bridge, I threw my cellphone overboard and shouted, "Ah ha, I'm free!"

I was getting Canada Pension and we could live economically on the boat, so I figured I could just take it easy in the summers and do a bit of work during the winters. The first summer, we slowly made our way up the coast visiting friends and relations and meeting new friends. We spent a lot of time in the Broughton Archipelago (three and a half months altogether). We meandered our way down the coast and wintered at the Madeira Park government dock in Pender Harbour.

I took a job doing some modifications on one of my thirty-twos, which went on for quite a while. It was good there, seeing a lot of old friends and having coffee at six in the morning at the Copper Sky coffee shop.

The next summer we headed north again, and on our return we stopped in Nanaimo for a while then went over to Bargain Bay and visited with good friends of my dad, Christa and Norbert Holm. They invited us to tie up at their float for the winter, which was great—good shelter, telephone to the float and they treated us like gold (wonderful people).

I did some renovations on a forty-foot sailboat for my friend Sandy Hately and did some repairs on other fishboats, including Sonny Reid's gillnetter *Instigator*, the boat I had designed for him many years before.

Then it was away north again. When we returned, we went back to Christa and Norbert's dock for the winter. By this time Li thought we should buy a house so that we would have a home and some security, so we started looking for a place. We looked all over: Pender, Sechelt, Westview, Comox, Port Alberni and finally settled for a house in Nanaimo, just a small place with a nice yard and fruit trees. We weren't using *Marana,* so we sold her and I took a twenty-eight-foot sailboat powered by an outboard for part payment. Li didn't like it, so I would go on trips by myself. I have to admit, it wasn't much of a boat. So I sold it and bought a twenty-eight-foot Grampian sailboat with a Volvo diesel in her. It was a better boat, but Li still didn't like it.

The Trip from Hell

One morning I had the Grampian tied up at Newcastle Marina in Nanaimo in a berth owned by a guy whose boat was out of the water (on the hard). His boat was going back in the water that morning, so I had to get out of his berth. When I turned on the TV to check the weather the screen was red and the ferries had quit running, but I had rented a berth in Ladysmith and had to go there, so I headed out. I had to hurry to catch the tide at Dodd Narrows and didn't have time to put on my rain gear. The wind was howling and halfway to the narrows it started to pour rain. I made it through the narrows, but the tide was running against the wind and it was blowing over fifty-five knots, so it was mighty rough. Although the Gulf Islands are relatively protected, it's a long reach to Ladysmith and it can get pretty rough. I just got through Dodd when my Livingston dingy capsized and was being towed with the bow straight down like a big scoop or a sea anchor. I was making about a knot and a half and smashing into the big seas, standing behind the wheel in the open cockpit soaked to the ass. I had trouble with algae in my fuel tank and the filter had been clogging up quite a bit. If my engine had stopped I would have been on the rocks and smashed up in no time, so I was really worried about that. Plus my cellphone had gotten soaking wet in my pocket and quit working. It took me over eight hours to get from Dodd Narrows to Ladysmith bucking into heavy seas, soaking wet, with gusts up to sixty knots. It was what you might call a trip from hell.

Buying One of My Own

Li was browsing the Internet and came across a thirty-seven-foot Farrell for sale at a really reasonable price. I looked at it and said, "Man, would I ever like to have her." I called the number and a boy answered. He said his parents were out, so I left a message. When the parents got the message, the wife said, "Wouldn't it be funny if it was Barrie Farrell?" Anyway, we went to Maple Bay to look at her. The owner, Brian Hebbert, brought her over to the government dock from the float at his dad's property where she was moored, and when I saw her coming, I knew I wanted her. They were all out of the same mould, but they all seem to look different. This one sat so pretty and proud-looking. It was built in 1976 as a pleasure boat and finished by DelDon Marine with a fish-boat cabin and a sailboat cabin over where the fish hold would be, with two big berths. She had a Perkins diesel and was well rigged and maintained. Li had figured out how much we could afford without borrowing from the bank, but the amount was so low that I was embarrassed to make Brian the offer. On the way home, Li could see the odd tear coming down my face and she felt sorry for me, but the amount of money we could spend was firm. I was sure Brian wouldn't come down that much in price, but I phoned him a week or so later and told him how much I could afford. I went through about three weeks of wanting the boat so bad and thinking there was no way I would get it. Then Brian phoned and said, "We sold my dad's property where I was mooring the boat and I'm going to have to pay moorage, so I really want to move it.

I was lucky to be able to buy the thirty-seven-foot Montagnais, *which I'd built in 1976. I have since renamed her* True North. PHOTO COURTESY BRIAN HEBBERT

Do you think you could come up with this much?" I said I was sorry but I couldn't come up with any more money. We talked for a while and then he said, "My wife and I talked it over and we'd really like to see you get the boat, so I'm going to let you have her for what you offered." Well, I could hardly believe it. I was fairly jumping for joy. I've got the boat and I'm now boat-satisfied for life. The name of the boat was *Montagnais*, but I'm changing it to *True North*, the name I kept when I sold the thirty-two Farrell that I built for myself almost thirty years ago. We put my Grampian sailboat up for sale on the net and the first guy who phoned bought it.

I recently penned a poem about cruising (my first stab at writing poetry). I sent it in to Rob Morris, the editor of *Western Mariner* magazine, and he published it in the January 2014 issue. Here it is:

Cruising

I love the sunrise on the ocean
I love the sunset too
I love to watch the changing weather
from rainbows to skies of blue
As I head my good ship *True North*
northwest along the shore I'll check the bays and
    inlets
that I love more and more
As I clear Vancouver Island, through Christy Pass
    to cross the sound
I'll just keep on a chugging cause I'm Alaska
    bound
I'll take my time to get there
Enjoying wildlife and hot springs too
and when it's calm and sunny the seas and skies
    are blue
Sometimes it's a little lumpy but that's all right
    with me
cause when I'm out there bouncing I still love the
    sea
I really like the north coast, there's peace and
    tranquility that's true
with whales, porpoises and sea birds and giant
    grizzlies too
Now you just can't beat the cruising on our lively
    BC coast
of its ruggedness and beauty we can surely boast

And when I get to heaven and look down on the
    ships
I'll say "hey" I've already been here on my Alaska
    trips

Singing Away

For the last few years I've been dabbling a bit in music. Although I don't play an instrument, I have a little studio and I sing (a cappella). I thought I'd try my hand at writing songs and I've written four in the last couple of years. The first one turned out the best, I think. It's called "Walking With You, Baby." I sent a CD to my country and folk musician friend, Alan Moberg, who lives on Salt Spring Island and has about sixteen albums out. He phoned me and said he didn't know what to expect when I said I'd written a song, but he was really surprised. He said it was a good song and he asked if he could record it. I said sure, I'd be flattered, so he took it to a professional studio and did it, and he did a nice job of it.

Anthony Alves also coached me and taught me a lot. He calls me his oldest student by far. He is a fine musician, composer and producer who started playing guitar at the age of three. He's now reproducing "Walking With You, Baby." I sang it in his great studio and he's adding all the different instruments and background harmony. Anthony is a multi-instrument player and creates information videos on how to use different programs, and also does music videos. He's coming out with an album of his own songs soon.

Recent Work

I've done a lot of work since we moved to Nanaimo—too boring to get into, but it's a big pile of work, and I also went over to Pender Harbour and worked. I'm going to get out of the fibreglassing business and I'm doing a lot of finishing now. I recently did finishing in Albert Bagshaw's boat, and built a dinghy bookshelf to stand in the corner of Eddy Hudson's condo with shelves in it to display his nautical artifacts. It's the first boat I've built for quite a few years. I've built a couple of cabins, but no complete boats. I finished it up the day before I had to go in for open-heart surgery. I had a triple bypass, a botched valve repair and a new valve (seven hours on the table). Li's looking after me and I'm healing up just fine.

Three years ago I got prostate cancer but they gave me two months of radiation and cooked that out of me, so I'm hoping for another twenty years or so.

My brother Keray passed away from a heart attack in April 2014. His daughter Lisa held a memorial for him at Palm Beach in Westview, near Powell River, and there was a lot of people there. Keray's sister-in-law Drewen Young gave a great eulogy. Keray's wife, Susan, put on another memorial at Pender Harbour and there was another large turnout. Jimmy Dougan, a well-known local character and musician, gave the eulogy and sang Keray's favourite song, "I Still Miss Someone," a Johnny Cash song. Whenever Keray walked in to a bar or wherever Jimmy was playing, Jimmy would stop what he was doing and play Keray's song.

Looking Back

I guess when I sum up my days of boat building, my favourite boats were my own thirty-two-footer *True North*; *Devil Woman,* which I built for Bud Kammerle; the boat I have now, the second *True North;* and the thirty-four-footer *Dieflyn* that I built for Dave Letson.

The hardest job I ever had was cutting the thirty-two up and making the plug for the thirty-four by twelve-foot mould when I was in North Vancouver—the mould that I hardly used.

Since I built my last boat, I've had a couple of "jobs from hell"—long ones. There were lots of unforeseen problems causing mountains of lousy fibreglass grinding and cutting in the hot sun. Another was a couple of months on my back and knees faring the bottom and

My son Allen and I, cutting the cake on my 80th birthday

lift strips, then faring the decks for weeks and weeks. Of course it doesn't help that I'm getting a little longer in the tooth.

All in all I've worked hard and put in long, long hours and ended up with very little to show for it, but I got a lot of satisfaction out of it. I've been lucky that my boats have turned out to be such a success—except my thirty-seven-footer that was tender in a bad following sea.

I have received a lot of recognition from my boat building.

I have a habit of when I'm asked a question and I'm not sure about the answer, I'll just say, "I don't know," not like some of the salesmen that come up with a cock-and-bull story that you can see right through. The only thing I'm really sure about is how little I do know compared to how much there is to know.

My memory for things that have happened in the past is really good. I can remember things from when I was two years old, and I can remember jokes that I heard sixty years ago and I can recall who told them to me. My short term isn't so great anymore. Sometimes I'll mention something that happened years ago to someone and they'll say, "No, that didn't happen." But every aspect of it is still clear in my mind and I'll be positive; if they don't remember, I just let it go.

I was at Newcastle Marina the other day and a guy said to me, "I just heard a story about you."

Len Stevens of Blue Wave Marine Surveyors had told it to me just after Hurricane Katrina in 2005. He had gone down to New Orleans to survey a boat and when he got to the marina the manager came out and said, "You see that harbour out there? Several hundred boats and they all sank except for one. You probably know the guy that built it. His name is Farrell." Ha! Ha! Good story, must have been some kind of fluke.

Yes I've had many ups and downs (more than I've mentioned in this book) but all in all she's been a great life so far and I'm looking forward to quite a few more years with the 6:00 a.m. coffee gang at McDonald's, joke telling, singing, writing songs and poetry, working, travelling and keeping in touch with my good friends.

Index

Page numbers in **bold** refer to images

Index